THA] DIAꞰIᴇꜱ

C000201085

or

The anecdotes and adventures of a Third Hand

Being a personal account of life on a
Thames Sailing Barge today

Rita Phillips

A Heritage House Publication

The Thalatta Diaries

First published April 2006
ISBN 1.85215.1811

Printed by Hythe Offset, Colchester
Published by Heritage House (Publishers) Ltd.,
Steam Mill Road, Bradfield, Manningtree CO11 2QT
www.heritage-house.co.uk
e-mail:sales@heritage-house.co.uk

With additional material by Peter Phillips, Roger Davies
and Terry Palmer

Cover: Thalatta under sail (J. Brannigan) all other photo's
P. Phillips unless stated.

CONTENTS

Prologue

The Lady of the Lard

"ALL PRAISE THE GODDESS!". "All praise the Goddess of the Galley, Lady of the Lard"

So there I stood on the deck of a Thames Sailing Barge, in the River Blackwater in Essex. I have on the Skippers patchwork blanket as a cloak, draped around me over my work clothes, a deck scrubber as a sceptre and with a crown made from a hair-band and pink feathers. I am surrounded by a group of nine and ten year olds venerating me as their Goddess of the Galley.

For the past few minutes the school group had been face painting on deck. Actually it would be more accurate to say that they had been drawing all over their faces with black felt tip. Some had what seemed to be beards, others spots, still others just looked dirty. I knew that something was going on but I didn't know what.

All was revealed when the children produced their 'props' and dressed me up. The ship's Mate Roger, records all on the video for posterity. It is the last full day of the Schools Educational Cruise and they have decided to 'reward' me for my week's endeavours in the galley.

Once fully attired in my "Goddess" regalia I am ushered down the companionway to the hold below. Roger videos me disappearing downwards like Orpheus into the Underworld but with the accompaniment of a dozen school children chanting "All hail the Goddess", once more.

Eventually we settle around the dinner table for our evening meal. Unfortunately tonight this is spaghetti! Most of the children make a fair attempt at eating the long strings of pasta much to their own amusement. Eventually, however, for the benefit of those who are not so successful I have to try to demonstrate how it should

4

be done. My pathetic efforts are once more accompanied by the worship of my new subjects.

Someone chimes in with "it's time to sing a hymn to the Goddess." I now get to see the significance of the urchin like makeup as everyone bursts into a very well rehearsed version of "Food, glorious food", from the musical *Oliver*. I can only lean back with a regal smile and pronounce "I could get used to this." Roger just grunts "don't get too used to it", whilst Skipper Cyril chuckles quietly in the background.

'Goddess Of The Galley'

So overwhelmed am I by this demonstration of something or other that I dictate, "As a mark of my appreciation I hereby decree that tonight the adults shall do the washing up". This is, of course, greeted with cheers, at least from the children.

After dinner the children present each of the crew with a small gift. Mine is an apron inscribed with the words "Goddess of the Galley and Lady of the Lard". It is a treasured possession to this day.

So ends a brief but amusing example of one of those experiences which money cannot buy but which we have enjoyed while working with children on the Sailing Barge *Thalatta*. This took place during my first season as Third Hand.

Since this time we have had water fights a plenty, seen seals by the score, been to regattas, open days, and had a close encounter with a sight of yesteryear. We have even had a rescue at sea and the sighting of a so-called "Ghost Ship." I enjoy it all so much that I have run off to sea again each year since.

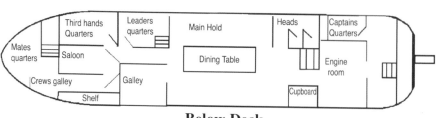

Below Deck

Chapter One

Of heads and hammocks

Our story starts in early April, a new year and with a new skipper but still the same enjoyment. I hope you find life on board *Thalatta* as wonderful as I do.

Monday

I should begin this day somewhere near the beginning. I'm Rita Phillips, Third Hand on the Sailing Barge *Thalatta,* and I'm one of the few sailormen in this job who wears a skirt; but *never* aboard ship.

The skipper of our crew is Kevin, with his six-foot-plus frame an imposing figure. On this, the occasion of our first trip of the season, our passengers are fifteen-year-olds, barely ten years his junior. Kevin, in addition to being the youngest current holder of a Skippers ticket for Sailing Barges, is also a champion "Mars" eater, the ship's supplies of these having to be kept hidden if we wish to have any left by the end of a trip.

Kevin is a mere boy compared with the rest of us, in his mid-twenties at the time of writing. Being the youngest current barge Skipper is no accident as he is dedicated to all things nautical. So dedicated in fact that he owns a veritable fleet of "winter project" boats in various states of dilapidation. These are affectionately (?) known on board as *Kev's Navy*

Kevin's quiet, almost diffident manner contrasts with that of the more rugged and extrovert Roger, the mate. Mature and greying with a perpetual twinkle in his eye he is a natural storyteller and even manages to make the emergency drills seem interesting. At least, for the first ten times you hear them.

Roger, like my husband Peter is approaching

fifty, sadly from some distance away and from the wrong direction! My age of course is a state secret, let's just say that I am in the middle of Kev and Roger. (*Peter's note: 'Our ideas of the middle seem to differ'*)

We are all aboard the Sailing Barge *Thalatta,* official number 116179, a bowsprit barge of 67 Reg. tons, built of wood by W. B. McClearon at the Naval Dockyard, Harwich and first registered on February 6th 1906.

Thalatta is approximately 90 feet long with a beam of 21 ft 6 ins and draws 5-ft aft. She was designed to carry 150 tons of cargo and was originally ketch rigged as a "Boomie", that is, with a mainsail on a conventional boom at deck level. This rather than the familiar spritsail rig of today with the main and top sails being carried on a "Sprit" rising at an angle from the main mast, just above deck level and almost bisecting the angle between mast and deck.

Thalatta has had a number of owners over the years and carried a variety of cargoes around the English coast and across to the Continent. She now earns her living taking parties of young people on cruises under the flag of the East Coast Sail Trust.

Now we are up to date. More details about our history later, but for now here we are, Kevin, Roger and me aboard *Thalatta*, lying at her moorings in the muddy and aptly-named Blackwater River in Maldon, Essex, all eager to get our passengers ready for sea.

This first week's group is from Sweyne Park School, a state school from Rayleigh, which is only about 20 miles away, so at least they know the area. Some of our groups come from as far afield as Lancashire though these normally bring an interpreter with them!

I do the final shop for the voyage on the way in. Husband Peter and I did most of the shopping Saturday evening and these are the bits we forgot! When I arrive on board at 1100 Kevin is giving the deck a hose down and Roger is bringing on board the coal for our stove. I just have time to make a brew of tea once everything is finally stowed away.

Laden with luggage for the week our party arrived to board at 1300 this afternoon, pouring out of their minibus with all the eagerness of a party of explorers. I don't know what their first thoughts are when they see *Thalatta* with her black hull contrasting in the sunshine with her traditional light blue deck and varnished wooden Top and Mizzen masts. (The Main Mast is of steel, though under its paint it looks like wood!)

Most of the youngsters will never have seen a barge before and the great red sails for which they are famous will only be hinting at their glory, as they remain furled aloft for the time being. Perhaps like many, these people will ask questions about the large wooden leaf shaped *leeboards* on either side of the hull. These have been called everything from stabilisers to spare gangplanks by the uninitiated. They are however lowered on the leeward side of the barge when we are under sail and do the balancing job done by an external keel on lesser vessels.

The school party hit their first new experience very early as they made their way from the quay up the narrow aluminium gangplank taking them aboard. The mud looked very cold down there: after all, it's still early April.

Our first job is to get everyone and everything safely below deck. We have to show our guests the correct way to make their descent of the companionway - backwards - into the converted hold, which provides their accommodation for the week. We then form a human chain passing rucksacks and other luggage from deck to hold where everything is temporarily stowed anywhere out the way.

With everyone crowded in the hold it is time for introductions and briefing. When all our passengers, including the teachers, are sitting attentively round the long wooden dining table in the centre of the hold, Kevin launches into the safety talk. Paraphrased somewhat, the safety briefing goes as follows:

"Red lines on deck mark the areas where children are not allowed; we will talk about those more when we go up." He continues, "These danger areas are those where, when the sails are up, they may swing across the deck and knock someone into the water, or in the bows where there are no safety rails."

Having given a few moments for these dire warnings to sink in Kevin then moves on to the below deck areas.

"The crew's quarters are out of bounds at all times. The leader's cabin may be entered by invitation only and the galley, where you will do the cooking, only with the express permission of Rita."

The latter is sometimes accompanied by further dire warnings of the consequences of upsetting "she who is in charge of food" or some such. The occasional unsubtle humour does however help to illustrate an important safety point as our galley contains hazards for unwary or unsupervised fingers. "The engine room and fore hatch are also out of bounds at all times."

It is now time to demonstrate the fire bell and run through the drill if it sounds. "If the fire bell rings everyone *must* go up on deck immediately. The crew will get your life jackets for you. Do *not* come back below deck to get belongings or life jackets. As I say, the crew will get these for you".

Roger now gives a detailed demonstration of how to put on the life jackets. Each of our charges is now allocated a life jacket, which is adjusted to fit, large yellow oilskin wet-weather gear, and a big wooden sea chest in which to stow personal possessions, not to mention of course the cause of the greatest excitement - a hammock!

After the inevitable excitement dies down I promise I will show them how to use one, but not until bedtime or we will never prize them out!

When pointing out the location of the Heads (toilets) sometimes someone asks why they are so called. One of us will then explain that, "In the old sailing ships there were no toilets, only a board with a hole in it at the front or Head of the ship. Hence *heads*. Of course if a wave came along you then had the first *bidet!*"

Once all the safety and organisational briefing is out the way the teachers will sort out the children into teams, Port team and Starboard team. This is usually done on the basis of who gets on with whom.

We point out that throughout the week these two watches will take turns in doing the various chores required to run the barge. These include cooking meals, setting table and of course, washing up!

By the time everyone is settled in it is 1530 before we get under way. On this occasion Kevin and Roger do the work of casting off. This appears a complicated business perhaps to the uninitiated as we have four lines going to the Quayside.

The bowline and stern line are self-explanatory but the spring lines are less so. These run from the front of the barge to the quayside near the stern, whilst one secured near the stern of the barge runs to shore by the bow. This system secures the *Thalatta* to her mooring whilst allowing enough free play for the tide to come in and out.

Unless there is a friendly helper on shore it is the Mate's job to release the lines, Spring lines last, before leaping aboard. The lines are all secured by the easily released *Bowline* knot which was described to me something like the following;

"The rope goes like a rabbit, down the hole, round the tree, and back up through the hole". You will just have to imagine it I am afraid, as this is the best I can do in print!

This is in fact one of the few occasions on which we actually use knots on board, as for the most part the weight of sail would prevent any knot ever being undone! For this reason, ropes are usually wound in a figure eight round wooden cleats to secure them.

Today we set out as ever, just before high water. Thus we go out on the ebb tide, much better than fighting against an incoming one! We have the youngsters sitting on the hatch out of the way while we cast off. Once Roger has sorted out the lines it is my job to pull in the rubber tyres on ropes which act as fenders.

The hatch is, I should explain the cover that goes over what would have been the open cargo hold in *Thalatta's* trading days. This is now permanently covered with a wooden "roof" and looks from the side like a very low cabin.

As we make our way down river Roger organises two of the young crew to coil the ropes clockwise on the hatch. Ropes are always coiled this way to run with the twist or *lay* of the rope as it is made.

Back in the autumn, my husband Peter and I visited the naval dockyard at Chatham. Among the other attractions on view is the rope making shed where, for centuries, most of the Navy's rope was made. To see the different types of ropes and the ways they were made was fascinating, though sadly beyond the scope of this story. Incidentally the shed where it is made is so long that the workers used bicycles to get from one end to another!

Now it is time to get our two barge boats on board as up until now they have been in the water, towed behind the barge. With the barge stopped, the davits are swung out and secured, then the boats are hauled from the stern up alongside the davits just forward of half way along *Thalatta's* side.

When the boat lines are secured to cleats on board Roger jumps in and I pass down a block and hook. This is attached to a chain in the front of the dinghy. I then pass down a second block and hook which goes to a chain at the back of the dinghy Not rocket science, but it works!

With everything secured Roger climbs back on board. Kevin now sorts the crew out into their two teams, one on each davit and with the traditional "Two six heave", every one hauls away until the boats are high enough to be secured safely on the davits by Roger and Kevin. This is one of the few jobs on board I am not strong enough to do except in an emergency.

Today we are motoring under the power of our big diesel engine. Were we not doing so, the teams would have been organised in the same way to haul up the sails. The cry of "Two six heave" comes from the days of the six man naval gun crews, each of whom would have had a number and a corresponding job. It was the job of numbers two and six to heave the cannon back into its firing position after reloading.

We make our way down to Osea Island and drop anchor for the night (standard admiralty pattern I am afraid, nothing fancy). Osea Island is as far as we can reach safely before running out of water if we leave on a high tide rather than "Punching" against an incoming tide. We do always, however, make sure that we lay out enough chain for the weather conditions. If as tonight it is likely to be windy and rough we lay out a little extra to put more weight on the riverbed. We may also give the engine a burst in reverse to help the anchor grip the bottom. Oh, and for good luck, we have to allow enough to cope with the coming in and going out of the tide. It's a good job the boys know what they are doing!

When judging how much chain to lay out it is always worth remembering that what goes down must come up! Coming up involves being wound up by hand, Good exercise for Captain and Mate, hard work for our young crews. Thus for the first time this year we leave behind our home port of Maldon tucked away on the River Blackwater on the east coast of Essex.

But enough of the reverie, it's time to get dinner organised. This will be the first meal prepared by the school party, as they brought sandwiches with them for lunch.

Tonight it is the Port team's turn to do dinner. Taking their numbers from those on their sea chests, one and two are on duty peeling and preparing the carrots and potatoes then placing them in saucepans on the six ringed gas stove which cooks all our meals. When the vegetables are on, knives, forks and spoons must be set around the table, together with beakers for the fruit juice. If I need any other help preparing the meat or vegetable dishes the youngsters will provide this as well.

Once the meal is prepared Roger and I serve it up.

On completion, the rest of Port team will do the washing up under my strict supervision. We have two sinks in which to do the washing up using hot water from the giant kettle that has been simmering away on the stove while we are eating.

We have to be very careful with our use of fresh water; the notices over the sink warning against waste are not there for effect! We have only the water we can carry in our two onboard tanks, use it all up and we are dry until we can get into port!

Although it has been another cold, windy day everyone seems to have enjoyed him or herself. Down below in the evening we are very glad of the heat from our coal stove in the corner of the hold as Kevin leads the children through the filling in of their daily Log sheets.

We issue these logs at the start of the trip and they are an important educational tool as well as an amusement. They contain information on such differing subjects as tides, navigation, knots and weather, all of which are vital for aspiring young sailors. Kevin supplies daily information as to where we have been, wind speeds and navigational points to notice such as buoys passed, so that everyone can keep a permanent daily record of the voyage.

Now we have come to the time of day so many have been waiting for getting in the hammocks! Probably the best way for me to explain how I show people the correct way to use the hammocks is to run through the drill, which goes more or less, like this.

"Right. Now I am going to show you how to get into the hammocks. First, who is sleeping in this hammock tonight?" (I usually pick on number three because it is half way along the side of the hold and easy for us all to see.)

"OK. Where is your sleeping bag?" When this is produced, I proceed. "All your hammocks are tied up by a rope with a loop and a bit hanging down. Pull the bit that is hanging down like this- the hammock then comes down so that you can reach it."

Having demonstrated, I open the hammock out to show them the contents.

"When you open your hammock you will find that it contains one mattress, one pillow and a piece of wood which we call a spreader. This fits in the cords at the head of the hammock and holds it open so that it does not smother you!" I now put the sleeping bag into the hammock and open it up ready for use, I then continue to demonstrate.

"Right. Watch now. You step onto your sea chest like this, so, with your back to the hammock. Then put your bum, bottom, backside or whatever else you want to call it into the middle." I demonstrate.

"Now, holding the rope above your hammock you swing yourself round until you are in the laying position. You zip yourself up like this, then you say Good night. Good night!" I then proceed to snore briefly!

"In the morning you unzip the sleeping bag, pull yourself up on the rope, swing yourself round and then get up!" Once more I demonstrate, although I suspect that getting up may come less naturally to some than going to sleep!

"Now you have to make your bed! You stick your sleeping bag in the hammock, take the spreader out, fold the hammock over itself, then take the rope down and round and under the canvas and through the shackle. Pull on it and you see that the whole thing goes back up where it came from. Make a loop, loop again to secure it and there you are!"

Sleeping arrangement demonstrations over, my official duties for the day are finished, though I usually chat for a while before disappearing to my cabin for the night. Tonight while Kevin is busy in the hold, Roger and I adjourn to our respective cabins.

The day has been cold and windy as you would often get this early in April in this part of the world. I do not go up on deck to ring Peter, as I am sure he can survive without my company for one night. Probably watching cricket on telly anyway. In a couple of weeks time I will have to compete with the seductive charms of the local cricket square if I want to get in touch with him!

I use a green plastic stool as a step to get me up into my bunk. This is just big enough for me to fit into, well wrapped up against the cold. When settled in I can't reach the door to close it so this has to be done before climbing in.

Before I settle down for the night I make entries for the day in the diary which I have been keeping of the season and which forms the basis of this narrative.

Winds Dropped

Chapter Two

The Third Hand

Tuesday, very early in April!

We get up early today after differing nights of sleep. The crew and the group's teacher all sleep well as do most of the youngsters, but some keep waking up, either being unused to these sleeping arrangements or just too excited still to settle.

After breakfast it is the Starboard team's turn to squeeze into our small galley to wash up while the Port team goes up on deck to raise the anchor. These lads are big enough to raise our heavy anchors, turning the handles either end of the windlass without any help. Younger groups need Roger or Kevin to lend some muscle. (I once asked what the anchors weighed. "A lot" was a rough translation of the answer!)

This morning we make our way to Rowhedge where we anchor for about one-and-a-half hours. Kevin and Roger ferry us all ashore in our two boats, lowering them into the water being the reverse of the procedure yesterday, when we raised them onto the davits. There is the additional task however that Kevin and I have to perform, in passing down the small outboard motors for Roger to secure to the boat's sterns. These motors are kept in the hold when not in use.

While ashore everyone gets the chance to spend some time having a good look round before returning on board.

We now make our way further down river to anchor for the night at Brightlingsea. We are under sail now and Port watch have the excitement of being on deck helping to raise or lower sail as necessary to maintain our progress.

I spend most of the day below deck doing various chores, including giving another demonstration of the use of the *Heads*. This involves letting water into the bowl by depressing a metal plunger on the top of the cistern, easy enough for this age group but sometimes tougher for the younger ones. Often one of the crew has to help with this. Oh joy!

There is a large lever coming up from next to the pedestal, looking a bit like a handbrake lever. This is pumped up and down vigorously to discharge the waste out into the river! To allow the system to work properly, we can only have that hard shiny toilet paper on board which adds to the pleasure of the whole operation!

This evening Starboard watch have the less than exciting but important job of preparing the dinner under my supervision.

The menu changes daily though it follows the same pattern every week thus making shopping for the ships stores relatively easy *(Peter's note: No it does not. It makes shopping for the ship's stores possible. There is nothing easy about spending two hours round Tesco's doing the "barge shop"!)*

Once the evening chores are done, washing up supervised, Logs completed and everyone in hammocks, I am glad to retire once more to my cabin. Too tired tonight to write my diary fully I reflect on how lucky I am to have such a job that I love so much and how on earth I got myself here!

It was of course all my husband Peter's fault.

One cold but bright late February afternoon Peter and I decided to take a walk along Maldon "Prom" rather than our customary constitutional round the Tollesbury sea wall.

We had hoped the ice cream kiosk might be open (somewhat optimistic for February but there you are.) Disappointed in this endeavour we decided to have a stroll along the quay to have a look at the assorted vessels wintering there. Having always been interested in anything connected with the sea I wander ahead. Peter, who's interests tend to be more aeronautical meanders behind.

Peter knows that I am looking for a change from my present job driving a mini bus for an old peoples home. Peter also reads everything he sees! Suddenly my attention is grabbed by a shout of "Hey Rita. Here's a job you can do!" Somewhat warily, I walk back to where he is pointing to a notice pinned to a shed. On reading the notice I see that it is advertising a vacancy for something called a "Third Hand" on one of the sailing Barges.

I am reluctant to take this seriously at first, as we have no idea how many weeks, months or years the notice has been there. The job will have gone by now. In any case I have no experience of working on any sort of ship never mind one of these historic sailing barges. To date my nautical ventures have been restricted to a few hours playing about in a small motor boat we once owned and an exciting cruise to North Africa with the Girls' Nautical Training Corps on the *SS Uganda* many years ago.

It is tempting, and the matter is clinched when Peter offers to write the application letter for me. This he volunteers for because he is more used to writing such things than I am. Also because he likes playing with the computer more than I. (He will however have to put up with endless teasing from various people about having only written it to get rid of me!)

The letter sent, we wait to see if there is any sort

of reply. Much to our surprise I am shortly invited to an interview on board the Sailing Barge *Thalatta!*

The fateful day arrives and at 1700 I board the barge to be greeted by Joe Brannigan the East Coast Sail Trust Chairman. He introduces me to Cyril the Skipper and to Roger the Mate. Joe also explains about the set up of the Trust.

A registered charity established in 1971 by the late John Kemp and the late Jane Benham MBE, it evolved from the Sail Trust of 1961. The trust now exists to preserve and maintain the Thames Sailing Barge *Thalatta* and by sailing her as a school ship, introducing young people to the delights and challenges of working on a traditional sailing vessel. He tells me that four Trustees supported by an appeals committee of two run the trust.

Introductions having been completed, we sit in the hold and I am duly "interviewed". The questioning is gentle and seems to take great regard to my ability to cook for a dozen people, though my maritime knowledge, or lack of it, is expertly exposed when Roger asks me what the bowsprit is!

I instantly take a liking to the people I may be working with. They are friendly and full of humour. The surroundings are less impressive with bits of lavatory (Heads) lying around, together with sundry ropes, boxes, and paint tins etc. *Thalatta* is only just starting to wake up from hibernation.

I arrive home to find Peter and Kim, our younger daughter, peering out of the window to see how I have got on. I am told I had a big grin on my face. True or not, I certainly had when a few days later I received a phone call from Joe telling me that I had got the job and that henceforth I would be something called a "Third Hand".

Cyril left as Captain at the end of my first season

(no connection), to be replaced by Kevin.

Now it is time to go back to my diary.

Wednesday

We all get a lay in today, as we have a late breakfast at 0900. Roger and Kevin take the group to Brightlingsea this morning for a look round and everyone piles excitedly into the ship's boats for the short trip. Once in Brightlingsea the children have the chance to take in the sights of this historic town with its links to both Bronze Age settlements and Roman fortifications.

The plentiful supplies of shellfish which first attracted our Bronze age forefathers continued to influence the growth of the town until recent times, combining with an excellent natural harbour to develop both oyster fishing and boat building industries.

I stay on board with Michaela, one of our young charges, who is not feeling well so does not want to go ashore. We amuse ourselves by making lemon meringue pie and then by preparing the sandwiches for lunch. When the others return at 1300 I am on deck laying in wait with the water guns and balloons. We have quite an extensive armoury of water guns and the crew is well drilled in their use! Water fights are an established part of the routine and (usually) enjoyed by all! Today a suitable ambush is carried out and all are wet but happy when those in the boats finally make it back onto *Thalatta*.

After lunch the whole crew except for Michaela and I disappear in the boats again. We enjoy ourselves cleaning some of the large amounts of brass on board and when the sun shines on the brass on the ship's wheel, compass binnacle and skylight surrounds, it makes all the elbow grease well worth while.

When the boats return once more it is reported that one party had seen a seal at close quarters. This is always exciting for the youngsters in our groups and is one of the main topics of conversation for the rest of the day.

Once back on board again two of the boys prepare dinner and greatly enjoy doing so. As ever, I wonder if they would enjoy doing this so much at home. If indeed, they ever contemplated preparing a proper meal.

Thursday

We have a late start again today with breakfast at 0900. The weather is still cold and miserable and no one is in too much of a hurry to go anywhere outside. The large wooden table in the hold makes an ideal table tennis table and our young crew members amuse themselves exercising their skills until lunchtime.

After a delicious lunch of bread rolls the kids are ordered up on deck and with some more "Two six heave", the young crew hoist the sails and do some real sailing. This is greeted with traditional April weather of hailstones and sleet. Never mind, we throw a few water bombs at each other anyway just for fun.

Once under way we set our crew to work scrubbing the deck while Roger and Kevin rig up the fire Pump. This not only tests the pump once more but also gives me the chance to soak all the kids! (*Peter's note: From personal experience later in the summer, I do not believe for one minute the pump needed testing. Any excuse to soak anyone is always welcomed!*)

Surviving the initial shock of their unexpected cold shower everyone realises that it is actually really quite fun. (*Especially Rita, see Peter's note above*)!

After an hour or so of enjoyable sailing and soaking, the wind drops and so it is all hands to lowering and stowing the sails. Although spritsail rigged barges became popular because they could safely be sailed by a man and boy, (sometimes with a third hand as cook) it is possible with a bit of organisation, to work it so that all

23

our young sailors have something to hold, haul or heave. Once all the exertions are complete, everybody is wet, chilled, and very glad of a good excuse to go below for a hot drink and cake.

Warmed and refreshed we motor up to Mayland Creek on the south bank of the Blackwater where we are lucky enough to see two seals frolicking and kissing near the Beach. We drop anchor off Osea Island at around 1730. After dinner everyone retires to bed at 2200 tired and happy. Although we are only ten miles or so from Chelmsford, the county town of Essex, we could indeed be in a different world.

Friday

A short day today as our youngsters leave early. Everybody is scurrying around emptying sea chests and filling luggage bags. The teacher and some of the children visit me in my lair in the Saloon. This serves as our souvenir shop and there are sweatshirts, caps, mugs, pencils and other souvenirs available to purchase as reminders of their trip.

It is important that all and sundry help in the tidying up process, so soon there are brushes and brooms flying around the hold. Metaphorically of course- no witches here!

Once the cleaning is complete it is time for the presentation ceremony. Every youngster coming aboard receives a signed certificate from the Skipper setting out the work that he or she has carried out as part of the crew, the ports called at and the miles covered on the trip. These certificates can then form part of the individuals' School Achievement Record.

The presentation itself is carried out on deck in nice weather, often finishing with a group photo of everyone sitting on the main horse. The horse is the wooden beam going across the deck to which the mainsail is attached by a large iron ring, called a traveller, when set. Its secondary function is as a very convenient seat, except if you're going about or gybing!

With formalities over everyone waits for the minibus to arrive to take them home. We have the usual mixed emotions as although most of the youngsters are naturally keen to see home and loved ones again, no one wants to leave the barge. The week has been a busy one much enjoyed, though the weather could have been kinder.

In the evening Peter takes me to our local British Legion Club where we share a "Murphy's" or three with friends. One of whom, Robin (later to become a keen Day Sail "Fourth Hand") asks whether all that hard work at the beginning of the year had been worth it? I think back to the beginning of February and the thoughts I had written down at the time.

The Hatch

Chapter Three

All that hard work

Wednesday, early February

It seemed a long time since our end of sailing season drink at Woolverstone last year and the cold hours we had spent subsequently putting our barge into hibernation for the winter. *Thalatta* had passed the time since, moored at Maldon quay, with everything possible stowed below decks. Just another old barge laying in the mud perhaps at first glance. It was now time to transform her once more into a working barge before our first young "Crew" would come on board in late April.

I arrived on board at 0900. This was my first day back for the new season (two days after the others, I have been working)! Kevin, our new Skipper, was there to meet me. After the customary brew, we took ropes, block and cable up on deck and placed them on the fore hatch.

When Roger, the Mate arrived it was more tea, any excuse, after which I started sanding blocks ready for painting. The rest of the morning was spent sorting and painting rigging.

Joe, The East Coast Sail Trust Chairman arrived mid-morning and I went shopping for bacon, eggs and bread, which was gratefully consumed, for lunch. After lunch Joe went to Brightlingsea to collect the materials for dressing the sails while we continued painting. Peter came on board about 1630 on his way home from work, which gave Kevin an excuse to make another pot of tea! We finished painting about 1700 and Roger and I made our ways home whilst the Skipper spent the night on board. (*Peter's note: I arrive to find Thalatta moored third Barge out and cross a gangplank to get onto the first Barge, no problem. However, the next bit is not so easy as there is no gangplank between this barge and my destination. Climb on board very carefully so as not to either dirty my suit (not the right kit, but some of us have to work for a living!) or make a fool of my self slipping and breaking something.*

Once safely on board I find Roger painting chains, Rita is painting her gloves and Joe having a smoke. I am pleased to meet Kevin the new Skipper for the first time. He is the only one doing anything important as he has the kettle on.

It's good to see Rita with her summer family and to meet up with Joe and Roger again.)

The next day we dressed the sails. The weather was fine so Kevin and I started laying the sails out on the quayside. Roger arrived just before 1000 and Joe arrived just after we start.

All four of us then armed ourselves with brooms and bowls, brushing on the dye which would preserve the sails against the sun light and keep them waterproof. It also gives them the distinctive "red" appearance for which the Thames barges are famous. Now purchased "Off the Shelf", this mixture was once made from such delightful ingredients as horses urine and whale fat among others! Although these charming raw materials of old were both effective and traditional, Peter has expressed an unhealthy interest in how anyone actually thought of mixing these ingredients together in the first place!

Roger had warned me before we started, to wear old boots, as they are inclined to get dressed along with the sails. He is proved to be right! We were all told to avoid applying the dressing too thickly as it would not dry evenly or quickly. Some puddles did appear and Roger, Kevin and I seemed, at one point, to be in danger of being cut off in the middle of the mainsail. Joe as ever, was enthusiasm itself.

The afternoon was spent trying to get the sails finished and packed. We succeeded except for two, which were still wet, Kevin put these away later. The next day I helped Kevin spread the sails out on the quay so that we could dress the other sides. This job took Roger, Kevin and myself all day.

The crew from the *Xylonite,* one of our sister barges were also dressing their sails on the quayside. They managed to enlist the help of some small boys who had the time of their lives with brush and pail.

Monday-late February

Roger spent most of the day painting the Leaders cabin while Kevin was busy fitting new gears to the windlass used for raising and lowering the anchor.

After having found the key to the big brass ship's clock and getting it going for the first time this season, I gave the focs'l a wash and thorough clean.

Mo, our visiting engineer spent the day hard at work on the Diesel engine, which we use for power when not under sail. Cyril, last year's skipper referred to this, somewhat scathingly as the "Iron topsail" and stuck to sail whenever he could.

By lunchtime, the tide had come in, floating the barge. This was important, as in the afternoon we had to lower the main mast ready to attach the sails and rigging.

When *Thalatta* rests on the mud, she is not level as she is when floating. To try to lower the mast when the deck is at an angle would make a tricky job downright difficult as it is considered bad manners to destroy aerials and mizzen masts, (especially our own), in the process.

Tuesday

I spent the morning scrubbing the forward galley after which I do the fourth hands bunk area, known as "the shelf" because of its shape and size, which, if one is being generous, could be said to be about the size of the average...shelf!

Wednesday

This was Galley day. I spent most of my time cleaning the walls, ceiling and worktops, the cooker also needed a good sort out. However carefully we put things to bed for the winter, everything always seems to accumulate dirt and muck between seasons. The Galley is very much my domain and must be kept in top condition throughout the season for the hygiene and happiness of all, especially the Crew.

After lunch Kevin and Roger carried the main sail from the quayside and spent the rest of the afternoon attaching it to the main mast with what, to me, appeared to be a complicated collection or ropes and rings. To the initiated this represents a simple and practical system for working our canvas.

Thursday

When I arrived in the morning, the sun was shining and it felt quite warm for a February day, which was good since we were preparing the rest of the rigging. Kevin gave me an oilcan with which to lubricate any bits requiring freeing up. Seeing me armed with an oilcan Roger chirped up with "who let her loose with anything squirty". I was shocked, but had to content myself with oiling all the blocks I could find.

After lunch Kevin and Roger put the tops'l on and it was my job to put boiled Linseed oil on all the cables to help preserve them. Kevin asked me to put some on the fore stay and I had to ask him what that was. He explained that it is the very large cable on which the fore sail runs up and down.

(Peter's note: I arrive mid-afternoon to collect some brochures to leave in Cathy Peachey's wool shop (one of my customers).

I find that I have timed this well as Roger produces a cup of tea and we all sit on deck sunning ourselves.

It would be easy to imagine it a June afternoon as we sit nestled among the other barges on the waterfront. I recognise the Xylonite two barges out but cannot see the name of the one between us, which is, to me, unusual, as it has no bowsprit.

The illusion of the summer season is spoilt by the confusion of mast, sprit and rigging as these lay flush to the deck as the sails are fitted. This also renders any kind of movement from one part of the Barge to another a precarious and complicated procedure for those of us not accustomed to climbing over and around cables and ropes.)

Friday

The boys greeted me with the judgement that it is "not so warm this morning". I thought that perhaps this was a good thing, as there was heavy work to be done. Roger, Kevin, Gary Diddams, a former skipper and now an adviser to the Trust, Richard and Grant, Skipper and Mate from the *Xylonite*, Nick and Joe were getting ready to raise the main mast using the windlass. Even with four people this is always hard work. Kevin and Roger keep checking the ropes and cables to make sure they do not become tangled or the wrong way round. Joe was on the quay releasing the wang so that the sprit stayed in the right place. After much effort and care the main mast was eventually in position. Nobody, by now, complaining of being chilly.

30

I watched proceedings from the *Lady Jean*, another of the Maldon sailing barges, this being the safest place for me as I was well out of the way. There is a lot of weight in masts and sails if they fall on you should anything go wrong.

Monday the first in March

When I arrived for the start of the week I was struck by how magnificent our barge looked as I saw that her freshly dressed, Main, Fore and Topsails were all fully deployed. *Thalatta* is as keen to get to sea as we are.

Roger prepared the first brew and while this was being drunk it was decided that painting would be the order of the day. Roger would finish painting the Leaders' cabin while I could make a start on mine.

Before we started painting there was some debate between Kevin, Roger and myself as to the positioning of the reading light in my cabin. The upshot being that the light was moved to the head of my bunk, instead of down by my feet.

Once the dilemma of the light was settled we commenced painting about 1130. This I did for the rest of the day with only a break for the customary lunch and brews. Roger on the other hand had, from time to time, to take a break from his artwork to assist Kevin rigging the Mizzen sail and Gaff.

Tuesday

While we sat on the keelson (the metal backbone of the barge) having our first cup of tea, Kevin's dad Alec appeared. Unbeknown to me, he had been working in the stern. It was Alec who gave me my first opportunity of the season to practice my newly certificated first aid skills as he later appeared with blood dripping from a gashed finger. This I duly cleaned and dressed while giving a running commentary. The patient miraculously survived despite this so I felt suitably pleased with myself.

Our first booking we were told today is now April 7th, a week earlier than anticipated. We would have to get a move on as we still had much to paint and clean and the engine was still in pieces undergoing maintenance.

Thursday March
Painting

Friday March
More painting

Monday, early March
Kevin asked me to put the Focs'l and Saloon "back together" as he put it. This meant getting the Clock and Barometer back on the wall and getting out the pictures and books.

We had a message this morning that Mo, our engineer had recovered from the illness which had kept him away from the barge for the last week, and he would soon be returning on board to finish work on the engine. Our "Iron Tops'l" had now been in pieces so long that we decided to put a picture of Mo on it to remind us what he looks like.

Tuesday
I pottered about for the morning. After lunch I got out the scraper and started work removing the flaking paint from the keelson. After the mid afternoon brew I was able to prime the Keelson whilst the others finished off their painting. I was also very ready for that cup of tea.

Wednesday
I put the Galley back together while Roger took the shields and plaques off the Coamings which go round

the saloon. These "trophies" have been given to us by different schools, which have been on the five-day trips with us. So far we have over thirty.

Thursday

I spent the morning sorting out the games cupboard whilst Roger painted and Kevin worked on the Quay sanding the dinghies, or barge boats as we know them, ready for painting. Watching them I think back to my first adventure with these small craft.

The Iron Tops'l

Chapter Four

More preparation and Rita goes solo!

My first experience of sailing the barge boats by myself had taken place the first year I was aboard with Cyril as Skipper.

On the way from the barge to the shore at Brightlingsea with our group of children Cyril had started to explain how to operate and steer with the little 4hp Mercury outboards which power the two boats. On the return journey Cyril had gone over the starting procedure again and added the dark aside that "the only way to learn is to practice!"

Once safely back alongside *Thalatta* Cyril had as usual seen all the children safely up the ladder and on board. When he himself stepped on to the ladder he kicked the boat away (with me in it!) with the comment "You can't trust me you know!"

So there I was slowly drifting away from the barge with no way of getting back without starting the engine and sailing my way back. Time to play. With a couple of smart pulls on the cord, the faithful outboard started. (Well it was faithful until someone dropped it over board a couple of years later!)

I steered a nice wide circle round the barge and felt really pleased with myself as I edged the dinghy back alongside, even managing to cut the motor at just the right time to nudge gently up against the ladder with my bow.

Whoosh! Then it happened. As if from nowhere a row of faces appeared over the edge of the barge and I was deluged with water bombs, super soakers and buckets of water, Cyril and Roger orchestrating the onslaught. So fierce was the bombardment that I was unable to secure the painter to the barge to tie up.

Undaunted, (well hardly), I restarted the engine and made one more careful circuit before, successfully this time, being allowed to return to the barge. Cyril graciously accepted the painter from me and a very wet and bedraggled Rita made her way up the ladder and onto *Thalatta*, very much to the mirth and amusement of the assembled multitude on board.

Once aboard I descended to the hold not returning on deck until I had loaded the two water pistols I keep below for such emergencies. Within five minutes I am pleased to say that the children had learned better than to mess with a "Woman Possessed."

Friday

Roger cleared the table in the hold ready to start preparing it for varnishing. Kevin was still on the Quay working on the boats. I spent the morning scraping the railings on deck.

By 1500 we were all up on deck to start the scraping ready for this season's coat of paint. Joe arrived and also joined in. By 1650 everyone had had enough and we called it a day.

We spent the weekend looking forward to more scraping on Monday...

Monday, mid March

My first job of the week was to paint the wooden box, which Joe had made to house the gas bottle. Meanwhile Roger was still sanding and varnishing the table, Joe sanded the bottoms of the boats and Kevin fitted some new stainless steel in the Galley. In the afternoon Roger prepared the ceiling for painting and, joy of joys, I went back to scraping rails.

Tuesday

Roger started by sanding the table down for another coat of varnish while I gave the gas bottle box another coat of gloss. Alec busied himself sanding rails ready for undercoating.

When I had finished the box I painted the windlass handles and then moved on to the bottoms of the boats. Worryingly, our engine was still in bits. We were definitely beginning to get nervous about that early start to the season!

Wednesday

There was much activity at the Quay this week as various Barges prepared their summer plumage. Yesterday the *Cabby* lowered her main mast for rigging whilst the *Xylonite* had her mast raised with her rigging now attached. Today the *Lady Jean* lowered her main mast in preparation. Amidst all the other Quayside activity, the *Hydrogen* moved back next to the *Thistle*.

My daughter Kim (aka "The Dart" because of her shape!) came on board and joined us for lunch at 1300. We again had lunch on deck in the warm spring sunshine.

After lunch Kim went back to college where she is studying travel and tourism. I painted, putting undercoat on the Main and Fore Horses then continuing with the red leading of the deck. Roger still worked on the table, sanding it ready for yet another coat of varnish.

(Peter's note: This evening Rita declares that she "may have caught the sun". She looks as though she has just got back from a Mediterranean holiday - someone is in the wrong job!)

Thursday

My morning consisted mainly of painting, the combings coming in for the Rita treatment. Roger puts his next coat of varnish on the table and Kevin, helped by Alec continued to work on the two barge boats.

After lunch I worked on the nameplates from the boats, sanding them and removing varnish in preparation for painting. Our dinghies are named "John" and "Jane" after John Kemp and Jane Benham MBE, two founding members of the East Coast Sail Trust. It was Skipper John Kemp in fact, who was instrumental in restoring a full rig of sails to *Thalatta* and fitting out her hold for occupation.

John was Skipper of *Thalatta* for many years and indeed died at the wheel on one of her trips. For a time after this tragic passing the barge had the brightly coloured paintwork on the hull painted out to give her the overall black scheme traditional for a barge "in mourning".

Jane was the daughter of the redoubtable author Hervey Benham, whose book "Down Tops'l" is to be heartily commended to anyone wishing to get a feel for the history and in trade workings of the Thames Barges.

Friday

By the time we pack up for the week we still have no engine.

(Peter's note: I ring home to let Rita know that I will be home from work just after 1800. I am informed that she needs to be taken to the British Legion for a pint or two of "Murphy's" as she has worked so hard in the hot sun. I am under-whelmed with sympathy but dutifully oblige anyway.)

Monday

Alec, Peter, an electrician and Roger all arrived within five minutes of each other. Jobs for the day were allocated, Kevin and Alec working on the boats, Peter electrics and Rita sorting out the five-gallon water containers. Roger was in his element sanding and undercoating the covering boards. (He is a sign writer by trade).

After yet another lunch sunning ourselves on the deck I sanded down the boat nameplates and gave them a coat of varnish, Roger primed some more of the deck and Kevin undercoated the boats.

We had some bad news in the afternoon. Our engine is not at all well and a part must be obtained from Scotland. I started to worry as it was now only two weeks to our first booking and whilst it would be both possible and perhaps romantic to operate under canvas only, it would not be very practicable. Kevin and Roger remained stoical.

Tuesday

Mo joined us late in the morning to do some more work on the engine. He was still trying to get over the flu and therefore did not feel well. Even his efforts would be in vain however if that darned part did not turn up soon!

About 1600 we had some fun and games as the *Cabby* needed to come off her moorings next to the quay. This meant that the *Nellie* and ourselves had to be moved out of the way. Since our engine was of course not working, the *Cabby* had to act like a tug using her power to manoeuvre the Nellie and us. We also attached a line to the *Lady Jean* and used our windlass to guide our stern when the *Cabby* pushed on our bow. Everything and everyone eventually is in position and secured, so that meant it was time for home.

Wednesday

When Mo arrived, mid-morning, we were all very relieved indeed, to see that at last he had our precious spare part for the engine. My delight, however, was slightly tarnished when I noticed that the hatch which I had taken so much care to wash thoroughly yesterday had now been unwashed by the seagulls. Next job then - clean it up again!

Thursday

I was the last to arrive today as I had gone shopping for the provisions. I hid the supply of Penguin biscuits. Kevin loves these biscuits and we would soon have none left if I did not take precautions!

James, a friend of Kevin's, arrived on board and helped me with my first job. This was tying the cords to the ends of the hammocks. This is a long job as there are about a dozen cords at each end of a hammock and twelve hammocks. This and putting in the spreaders took us all morning.

After lunch James and I carried the sea chests out from the leaders cabin, got out the oil skins and checked all the equipment on the life jackets before stowing everything in its rightful position for the coming season. Joe arrived mid-afternoon with the mattress covers; we put in the foam inserts and stowed the complete mattresses in the hammocks. Kim arrived just before 1600 in time to help and to scrounge a lift home with me. Mo spent all day tinkering with the engine, which he says, should be ready tomorrow.

Friday

Kevin and Roger spent most of the morning working up on deck. I sorted out the children's Log Sheets for the season. Kevin had been very specific in dictating how these should be done. By the end of the day the engine looked reassuringly intact.

Monday

As we were sailing for the first time next day, I was despatched to get the provisions for the three days of our trip. This little excursion will be just to make sure everything (and everyone) works OK. Kevin also hoped to beach at Goldhanger to paint the hull if the weather was favourable.

When I returned with the provisions Roger was painting the deck while Kevin and Alec tidied up the engine room. When all was tidy Kevin started the engine and generator. Both ran reassuringly smoothly, at least to my ears. We just had time to put the boats in the water before lunch.

After our lunch I sanded and varnished the nameplates and Gill Wood, our Trust Secretary, came on board to bring us more of the Log Sheets that the groups will use throughout the summer. By 1700 all was pronounced ready for our maiden voyage of the year.

Thus ended the transformation of our "ugly duckling" of the winter to our "graceful swan" of the summer. Now it just remained to be seen if everything worked as it should in time for our first young crew."

Between The Wars (E.C.S.T.)

Chapter Five
The battle of Felixstowe Dock

It is early April and our second week of sailing. This week's group is from the Hawthorn Preparatory School, just outside Redhill in Surrey.

Monday

Today sees us all arrive bright and early at the quayside. Kevin helps me stow the stores that Peter and I have purchased over the weekend. We manage to get everything put away, tinned food and cereals in the cupboard next to the galley, frozen items in the fridge and fresh fruit and vegetables (no scurvy on this trip!) in the little storage area in the Focs'l.

No sooner are we finished than this week's group arrives from Surrey. They have had the customary "interesting" journey round the M25. This group is younger than last week's, a mixed bunch of excited nine and ten year olds, which makes settling in and briefings that much more fun!

As usual there is much excitement at the prospect of climbing into and not falling out of the hammocks. I am firm. No one is allowed to try them out until the evening.

With formalities completed, we cast off from the quay mid-morning, motoring up to Osea Island before Roger lowers the anchor. The children are not allowed to lower our anchor, as it is too dangerous a job for the inexperienced. Carelessly or over enthusiastically used, the winch could run away with the weight of the anchor and chain and a finger in the wrong place would soon part company from its hand. Laying next to Osea Island we take our lunch, the children having brought sandwiches for this first meal. I however do prepare something for the crew.

As part of the normal briefing everyone is given a very short history of the *Thalatta* but often someone wants to know more. Such is the case today as Tim, the teacher, asks about the early life of our barge. I take him down to the saloon and give him a Trust leaflet describing *Thalatta's* early life. I also show them some of the early pictures of the barge, which we have there. These show how *Thalatta* looked when rigged as a boomie and as a motor barge. Both contrast with the grace and power of our craft in full sail today.

After lunch we motor our way down the River Blackwater before hoisting the sails to take advantage of some decent sailing weather. When we are off the power station at Bradwell a porpoise joins us briefly, much to everybody's delight, mine especially as I have never seen one before. After too brief a time our companion disappears and we are all left with just a unique memory.

We sail our way to Brightlingsea, where we anchor for the evening. Then it is the usual first night routine of logbook completion and hammock boarding instruction! When everyone has settled down I go up on deck to ring Peter.

"Hi you."

"Hi love. Where are you tonight then?"

"Three guesses."

"Brightlingsea?"

"Yup."

This will be the first of many such exchanges this summer!

Tuesday

We are up and away early. We use the engine to come out of Brightlingsea, which gives us a brief view of it's hilltop church of All Saints.It has a display of tiles in the nave, and a memorial to all the local men lost at sea, including one who went down with the *Titanic*. It is perhaps no bad thing to occasionally be reminded that there has to be a price paid by those who work on the water.

We continue to motor on past St. Osyth, though we can see nothing of the vast 12th century Abbey known as the Priory. We pass Clacton and up to Walton -on-the-Naze. Here we hoist the fors'l, tops'l and part of the mains'l ready to sail into Walton Backwaters. Unfortunately in hoisting the sails someone manages to damage the forward hatch cover and break off one of the pin rails used for securing the ropes! No one is telling me who the guilty party is!

By lunchtime we are safely anchored in the Backwaters, so Roger and Kevin are able to take the group ashore in one of the dinghies. The youngsters and the teacher enjoy themselves playing on the beach while our "Boys" dig for lugworms to use as bait for the evening's fishing.

From my vantage point on the deck of *Thalatta*, I can see our boys on one side of the river and the youngsters and teacher on the other side. As the tide goes out there is less and less water around the boat but more and more mud! Kevin and Roger, realising their predicament, abandon the lugworms (for now), and rapidly make their way back to the boat, but not as fast as the water leaves it!

We now have a potential problem. We have the group on one side of the riverbank with water. We have a dinghy the other side of the river bank, without water. Now while a barge boat may not look all that big and heavy, it is designed for floating on water, not for pushing across sticky Essex mud!

Just to make matters more interesting, I am on board the barge with another dinghy. I can lower this on the davits but the outboard motor is not fitted and it is too heavy for me to lift into the boat without a considerable risk of dropping it overboard.

While no one is in actual danger of anything worse than a boring wait, the situation is annoying. Fortunately Kevin and Roger realise what is going on before it gets to be too much of a problem, but they still have to struggle for three-quarters of an hour, manhandling the dinghy across the mud and chasing the receding tide. Eventually of course our heroes are victorious and off they float to bring everybody safely back on board.

In due course we all see the funny side of things, as we usually do, and all is well. It takes a little time though.

During dinner Kevin goes up on deck to check that everything is in order. Unfortunately, coming down the stairs he slips and descends, bump, bump painfully on his back. This causes great merriment all round as we have already briefed our group to do it backwards and Kevin was coming down front wards.   Kevin does well to turn this into a teaching point as to what can happen easily if you come down stairs the wrong way. (I should perhaps explain that the Crew sometimes do it the wrong way but we are used to going up and down all day).

Later in the evening one of the children injures his arm coming down in the same way and I have to do my nurse act, putting his arm in a sling for the night and dispensing sympathy. Some lessons are obviously only learned the hard way!

Everyone in bed by 2200 after an entertaining day enjoyed, (I think), by all. Though not, perhaps one of our more inspiring days.

Wednesday

After breakfast Kevin goes ashore in one of the barge boats to pick up our engineer Mo, who is needed to carry out some maintenance on our engine. When the taxi work is done, Kevin and Roger take everyone ashore to visit Walton. Roger stays ashore with the group while Kevin brings both dinghies back to the barge.

While this is going on I busy myself in the galley making cheesecake and sandwiches while Mo changes a filter on the engine. When Mo has finished Kevin takes him ashore again and collects the group at the same time. With them is young Andrew who has joined us late having been ill for the start of the trip.

By 1300 we are all able to enjoy our lunch of the sandwiches and cheesecake on deck. Lunch complete it's up anchor, set the sails and head towards Harwich and Felixstowe.

"Do you know where you are then Rita?" says Roger on our way.

"On a barge?" I reply hopefully, wondering where this is leading.

"Bloody Point."

"Pardon."

"Bloody Point. That's the name of this headland here, though it's not marked on many of the maps."

"Why is it called that?" I enquire.

"It's the site of the first sea battle recorded in British waters. It was fought between King Alfred and Guthrum, King of the Danelaw, and by all accounts it was very bloody. Hence the name".

"So who won?"

"Blowed if I know," replies Roger, "I wasn't there." Mine of information some people!

"There was of course a greater battle fought round here, you know," I grin.

"When?" queries our Mate.

"Don't you remember," I ask, "the Battle of

Felixstowe Docks?"

"So remind me," he prompts.

"Although the Battle of Maldon is well documented, one of the most closely contested sea battles of recent times, the Battle of Felixstowe Docks has not, as yet, been chronicled.

This was another of those little adventures, which took place when Cyril was Skipper in my first year on board.

We were innocently cruising around in the river opposite Felixstowe, admiring the many different coloured containers decorating the docks. Suddenly we spied the *Xylonite* coming up behind us. Now, even with both barges using the engines rather than being under sail, *Xylonite* is still the faster vessel. There was no escape! We are, however, the best armed barge on the East Coast so an interesting confrontation could be engineered.

As *Xylonite* overhauled us, Roger and Cyril busied themselves setting up our main armament, the "Funnaliser" (no I don't know why it is called that). This is a catapult made of four strong pieces of elastic stretched between the rigging and with a jug stolen from the Galley, used as a sling capable of shooting half a dozen water balloons fifty feet or more.

I loaded the super soakers and filled water balloons. Our young crew eagerly awaited their instructions. Within minutes the unsuspecting (maybe!) victim closed to within range. Roger began shooting the catapult with me keeping him supplied with ammunition from the bowl of water balloons which we had placed ready, next to the weapon.

We thus unleashed a hail of water balloons, which

was augmented by an excited bunch of kids manning the super soakers and throwing still more balloons!

The outgunned *Xylonite* had to be content with circling and returning fire with hand thrown wet tissue balls and any of our balloons which had not burst. Clearly they could not match us in weaponry and in a turning fight their speed was of no advantage.

For a quarter of an hour or so the barges circled each other, both Skippers displaying Nelson like seamanship to stay within range. Cyril ordered, "Don't shoot till you see the whites of their eyes" and Roger encouraged with, "Go on everyone let them have it"

Eventually, as though realising that they were outclassed, our opponents break out of the circle and head at full speed towards the west. Knowing that we cannot match the *Xylonite* for sheer speed we do not give chase but with much celebration from our young crew of "Pirates" resume a lazy course of our own in the opposite direction."

Story telling complete, we reach Shotley by the time we are ready to stop for the night.

This evening, two boys, Jamie and Andrew help me to prepare the meal. Our dinner consists of pizza and salad followed by more strawberry cheesecake. No scraps are left. This is perhaps a shame in some ways as after dinner the youngsters are able to spend some time on deck, crabbing, before coming down for "log time" with Kevin and lights out.

Thursday

We're up early this morning so that we can wind up the anchor before breakfast! Coming out into the channel as we leave Shotley the sea becomes very choppy and Roger is concerned for me. I am organising

47

the children washing up when he comes below and relieves me, sending me up on deck where I will be less susceptible to seasickness. Fortunately this is one malady with which I do not suffer, but I take the chance of enjoying a few minutes of the wind and spray in my face. Not something I get a lot of in the galley!

We make our way back past Walton, Clacton and Brightlingsea without stopping, as the weather is too rough here to take the boats ashore comfortably. We are able to drop anchor at Osea Island, in the Blackwater, as when we get there the wind has now dropped and it is nice enough for us to use the boats to get ashore so that we can picnic on the beach.

We are able to enjoy a pleasant lunch in the sunshine, after which, most of the children decide to go paddling. Alexandra and Tim however are adventurous (daft?) and decide to brave the April temperatures and have a swim. While this is going on Kevin and Roger organise a tug of war between Port and Starboard watches, which of course gives rise to much hilarity and amid which Starboard watch wins, we think!

It is not long before our intrepid swimmers decide that it is much more fun, and warmer, playing on the beach. They are, I think especially glad when by late afternoon it is time to go back on board for hot drinks all round. Everybody appreciated them, not least those members of the crew who are not as young as others.

Tonight, Alexandra and Emily prepare the dinner and we all enjoy their lasagne, peas and mash, despite the fact that we ran out of gas half way through the meal and the bottle had to be replaced. Try finding that in a cookbook! Afterwards some of the children purchase their gifts from our shop and most do some crabbing before Kevin gives his evening talk

View From The Wheel

General View Of The Hold

Mains'l Set

Friday

Today's first job is to make our way the short distance back to Maldon while the children prepare for their return home. They all have their bags packed and up on deck by 1100 then its time for them to sweep up the Hold and check all the boxes to make sure that nothing is left behind. Once this has been done the Hammocks are turned upside down so that no dust, sand, socks or stray crabs are left in them!

The group has its lunch up on deck, just before we arrive at the quay at 1230. When we get there, we have to wait for the *Alice* to move so that we can use her berth. All is settled and the group gets ashore by 1330. Then it's time for a final tidy up before I leave for home.

Chapter Six
Sea wall rendezvous and a "ghostly" encounter

This week our guests are from Wodensborough School, who call themselves "the boys from the Black Country." Husband Peter is graciously allowed to help me with a "Big shop" on the way to the barge this morning. This takes two full trolley loads. I don't think that he is over enthusiastic about this part of my job. (*Peter's note: My wife sometimes displays a unique talent for understatement.*)

We get everything aboard, with tins and dry goods in the cupboard in the hold, and frozen items in the fridge in the galley, but most importantly we have to keep the sweets and chocolate hidden from Kevin.

As usual today there has been some banter between Peter and myself about this part of my duties,

"The Trust is getting two for the price of one when it comes to doing the shopping."

"You don't have to help, I can do it."

"So how many trolleys can you push at one time?"

"I *could* get one of the boys to help."

"Yeah right," and so on.

Our Group for the week arrives on time and we set out at 1600 motoring down the Blackwater until we finally anchor for the evening at Pyefleet about a hundred yards off the East Mersea coast. Mersea Island is situated just south east of Colchester and separated from the rest of the county by a narrow strip of land known as the Strood. When there is a high spring tide the water covers the road and as the Islanders would put it, "The mainland is cut off."

I have a hospital appointment on Tuesday morning. This is a regular thing designed to keep tabs on the rheumatoid arthritis. Not that it affects work on board *Thalatta* much, though I try to avoid the "two six heave" routine except in an emergency.

So that I can make my appointment in plenty of time, after dinner, Kevin takes me ashore in one of the boats so that Peter can meet me with the car. We have reconnoitred the area on Sunday, so naturally I am on the beach while Peter is looking for me on the sea wall. Mobile phones are red hot and each blames the other! Eventually, as in all good stories there is a happy ending as we find each other and domestic bliss is (more or less) restored. Kevin is highly amused and does not let Peter forget the incident for the rest of the summer.

(Peter's note: Rita's navigation and direction giving are legendry. On this evening I arrive at dusk, park the car and walk the 400 yards to the sea wall across a field. Mobile phone calls are exchanges along the, "Where are you?" "We're here" and "where is here?" variety. It turns out Rita and Kev are walking along the beach in the opposite direction from me walking round the sea wall. While domestic harmony is eventually restored, two years later my reputation has not been!)

Tuesday

Peter gives me a lift to the hospital then runs me down to Mersea Stone where Kevin brings one of the boats ashore once more and picks me up to get me back on board by 1130. No communications problems this time. In the meantime Roger has been in left in charge of cooking breakfast for everyone. I will probably never know how, but he manages to get a tin of baked beans to explode making a nice mess all over the galley. Amateurs!

After lunch we motor down towards the river

51

Crouch before hoisting the sails and having a sail around. Anchoring mid-afternoon Kevin and Roger take the kids ashore to play cricket, thus proving we are civilised, while I stay on board and get dinner ready. We don't want any more amateur cooks today, do we?

After dinner I hear great cries of excitement coming from up on deck with numerous shouts of,

"I've got one."

"Mine's biggest,"

"Don't let it get away."

" Oh dash it."(I think!)

I know that our evening crabbers are at work, tossing their lines over the side baited with scraps from the galley to lure their prey. I go up to watch for a while as the noise level rises. The sum total of this entire endeavour is One crab. As I go back down below I pass comment to Roger. "Perhaps it is a good job Peter and I spent so long in Tesco's after all. If I relied on my "Hunter-gatherers" for food we would all starve."

We will perhaps gloss over the reply.

Wednesday

The next morning we start early, under sail before breakfast. We make our way out of the River Crouch to the accompaniment of the sound of the guns being tested at Shoeburyness. Their thunder gradually fades as we sail towards the River Colne. The wind is in the wrong direction today for their sound to annoy the good people of Clacton too much.

As we pass Buxey Sands there is a treat for the party as we spot a large number of seals basking in the sun. There is some competition to count them with various figures being put forward. We eventually agree to settle for forty-two.

We anchor for the night once more in the Pyefleet channel, where everyone except me goes ashore to Mersea Stone, the beach area of East Mersea, for more games on the sand. I remain behind, for in the absence of showers or bath on board, a wash down in a large bowl when no one is about is the best I can manage. It doesn't take much imagination perhaps to work out why this is known on board as a "Birdbath"!

Thursday

Today everyone buys something from our small gift shop which we run from the saloon just forward of the hold and right outside my cabin door! When the shopping is finished it is all ashore to Brightlingsea for a look around, a bit more shopping and some more games. I stay behind and sort out the takings and a list of items sold!

When I have finished my chores I go up on deck to wait for the others to return. While on deck I notice another barge in the distance. This in itself is not, of course, unusual but as I look at her I see that something looks wrong. At first I can't work out quite what, even through the binoculars. Then I realize, she is far too small!

As she comes closer I realise that I am seeing the *Cygnet* for the first time. This barge is only 25 tonnes as compared with our 90 and has a crew of only one. She is spending the summer sailing the local waters loaded with straw demonstrating the traditional way of carrying such a cargo. The straw filling her hold and rising up high above her deck gives the appearance of a floating haystack. Hence the traditional term "Stackie" for such a vessel. I go below to get both cameras, video and click-click. I get some nice shots of this beautiful little vessel as she sails by. Although small in comparison with most

53

of the other barges that still sail these waters she makes up for this lack of size with her grace and her evocative cargo.

Cygnet is also one of the few Barges around which is still steered by a tiller rather than a wheel. Accordingly her Mizzen is mounted on the rudderpost rather than inboard.

Sightings of the *Cygnet* have been reported in the local paper which has taken her unusual size and loading, together with the "now you see her, now you don't" nature of her voyages, and built the story of a "Marie Celeste" type ghost ship sailing these waters. (Which just proves that you should not believe all you read.) I am disturbed from my reverie when everyone returns on board in time for lunch. With the food finished and washing up done, we up anchor and head back towards Maldon. Tonight we have an early dinner, as the group needs to start packing ready for home time tomorrow.

Friday

Up early for breakfast at 0800 then we all set to, cleaning up the hold, hammocks and boxes. Clothes were all packed away last night. When the housework is complete we have the presentation of certificates for the week. Our guests then depart by coach and, after some last minute cleaning up, the crew departs as well. In our case, for the pub!

Monday, the last in April

This week's group is a Special needs group from Castle School in the Midlands. Special needs covers a variety of problems. The children could have behavioural difficulties, although not severe or this could represent a safety hazard. Some are Autistic to differing degrees and most have mental ages significantly less than their physical years.

All require some form of additional support. My involvement in this respect is mainly the provision of any special dietary requirements but this is also the time when my understanding and nurturing side sometimes comes into play. *(Peter's note: Oh is that when!)*

These groups can be hard work but are especially rewarding to work with and frequently give us some of our most enjoyable weeks. For a start there are no spoiled brats in these groups, and although sometimes the youngsters can of course be difficult, they cannot help it, and when they enjoy something they really show it.

I quote here from the alphabet that the kids drew in the crew logbook.

A	Anchor	N	Nautical
B	Beach	O	Octopus ??!!??
C	Captain	P	Pirates
D	Dinners	Q	Quiet
E	Engine	R	Rita and Roger
F	Fishing	S	Sun
G	Gulls	T	Thalatta
H	Hammocks	U	Underwater
I	Identification lights	V	Vang
J	Jib sail	W	Water
K	Kevin	X	Kisses
L	Life jackets	Y	Yellow painted boxes
M	Mr Haynes (teacher)	Z	Zzzzz - Goodnight

Interesting.

Everyone is safely aboard by 1430 and, once unpacked, they go for a walk up to Maldon. Watching them go, I pause to think once more how lucky I am to be doing the job I am doing. Roger appears next to me and we get to talking.

"You were at my interview, so you know how I got to be here. What got you involved with the *Thalatta*?" I ask Roger.

"Well, Rita," he replies, "I've always loved messing about in boats. My poor mother would have had kittens had she known that, at the age of twelve years old, when she thought I was round at a friend's house listening to records or talking football, as most of my mates were, I was in fact two miles off the coast fishing."

"How come?" I ask.

"A friend and I would push an old clinker dinghy down the beach and row off to fish for cod. No lifejackets, no compass, no flares. Not even, dare I say it, a mobile phone. Just an overwhelming urge to be on the water.

When I grew up I became a sign writer and worked at this for many years, though I still kept up the fishing and my love of boats. When at forty-nine years old I was offered the chance to be Mate aboard *Thalatta* I felt that I had finally found my destiny."

"What about all the kids?" I enquire.

"I have brought up two children and, like lots of fathers I suspect, missed chunks of their childhood through pressure of work. I now feel I've been given a second chance. I can be Grandad to groups of children every week. I can once again play silly games on the beach, have water fights and generally make an ass of myself without getting arrested."

"Will you always work here?"

"Well at fifty-eight now, I wonder how much longer I can carry on, the work aboard being strenuous to say the least at times, raising anchors, stowing sails and the hundred and one other little jobs there are to do in the cold and wet sometimes. But with the support of some top class skippers and crews I can think of no job I would rather do."

One way or another I manage to lose track of time and we have a late dinner!

After dinner I show the youngsters how to get into their hammocks as usual and we organise them ready for bed. This is to some extent a wasted exercise as we cast off from our mooring at 2200 to make our way down to Osea Island to drop anchor. Most of the children come up on deck in their pyjamas during this short trip and are much too excited for us to have any chance of getting them back into their hammocks until all is stowed away for the night.

Tuesday

Today is a quiet day as we are greeted with a strong, gusty wind when we awake. So we play safe and stay at anchor. We would have had to sail in the days when *Thalatta* was "in trade" carrying cargo. Then we may have been reliant on getting to port to pick up a cargo to make the difference between being paid and eating, or having to wait up on "starvation buoys" until a cargo became available. These days we have other considerations, especially with passengers aboard, and it is 1500 before the weather has relented enough for us to make our way up to the river Colne to anchor for the night.

While we have been waiting to set out, some of the children helped clean the brass while others occupied themselves crabbing. Once we are anchored in the Colne, Kevin and Roger take them ashore at Mersea Stone. Roger seizes the opportunity to go and dig for some bait!

After dinner Kevin and Roger settle down to some fishing from the deck. Roger, with the help of one of the boys, manages to catch an eel, Kevin manages to catch a "bird's nest" in his line. He spends some time trying to untangle the knots of fishing line, which, with a mind of their own have managed to form a replica of a nesting place. I try to help but eventually give up, so I go below and do not see if he has to cut the line to sort it all out.

"Thalatta" Pictured In 1964 (E.C.S.T.)

Chapter Seven
A fouled anchor

This Wednesday morning we have some fun and games, unintentionally! Everything starts as usual, up at 0800 for breakfast then tidy up the Galley and hold, all perfectly normal.

Then we have to weigh anchor. All goes well at the start, three-quarters of the way up however, the anchor decides that it does not want to come any further and slips back down again. This is not fun, since winding up the anchor and chain is heavy work even (or especially?) with our young crew helping.

We decide that the problem is an accumulation of mud on the windlass causing the chain to slip and this means cleaning the barrel around which the anchor chain is wound. We play the hose over this until the mud has been washed away. Finally after much effort, we manage to get the anchor up, but our victory over the mechanical fates is short lived since, after travelling for only a few yards, the engine promptly stops! The anchor is dropped back down again.

Kevin disappears below deck to whisper sweet nothings, dire threats and nautical incantations to the engine, and this works. (Or it may have been the spanner he took with him). So up comes the anchor, successfully this time and we are off. We eventually manage to reach Rowhedge, opposite historic Wivenhoe, where the Colne narrows.

The group goes ashore for a while to post cards and to visit the local shop. When they return we raise the anchor (no problems this time) and head for Pyefleet but the best laid plans of mice and bargemen and all that applies, for the weather now changes. With wind strengthening and rain coming nearly horizontal we have to make a decision: stick it out heroically for our original destination; or chicken out stoically and spend the night in the shelter of Osea Island. We go to Osea!

Two of the girls, Gurpreet and Kirsty, prepare us a nice dinner tonight, which we enjoy in the calm of the Blackwater off Osea, but we soon have two casualties to sickness, one during and one after dinner. Guess who cleans that up? - poor old Roger of course! All in all I am very pleased to get into my bunk this night and Peter has to go without his evening phone call.

(*Peter's note: Going for a walk around the sea wall I have the pleasure of watching as Thalatta motors up river, the white bow wave making an impressive sight as she battles her way against a brisk west wind. She looks to be going at a great rate of knots, though barely moving above walking pace relative to the land.*)

Thursday

We make our way from Osea Island up towards Maldon first thing in the morning. The trip takes us about an hour so we arrive at the quay nice and early. When we are safely tied up, Anna and John (the teachers) decide to take the children up to the town for lunch. While they were enjoying their chips and some shopping Roger, Kevin and I had a couple of hours to do some tidying up.

With everyone off enjoying themselves Roger and I both take the opportunity to go ashore and have a shower. This makes a very pleasant change from the "birdbaths" that I am used to at sea.

In the evening we enjoy a dinner of lasagne cooked by the boys. Washing up complete, I take the opportunity to surprise Peter and arrive home for a comfortable night in my own bed.

Friday

I return on board at 0700 before Kevin and Roger are up. I go into the main Hold and find that John is about so we have an early morning brew. After breakfast starts the big clean up, sleeping bags away, hammocks cleaned and general tidying up. While this is going on the coach arrives for our group and I make the driver a cup of tea. Final, tearful departure takes place at 1015. Some of the children become quite emotional. Everyone seems to have enjoyed the trip.

Later, John and Barry from the SS *Uganda* Trust come aboard. The Trust is one of our sponsors and they have come down to present us with a cheque. Fund raising is always an important matter for any charity. In our case we rely heavily on donations, sponsorship and open days apart from fees for schools and day sails.

I find this an interesting session as my first experience of life at sea was as a Sea Cadet on an educational cruise aboard the SS *Uganda*. Coincidentally, I discover that Barry was a Ship's Officer at this time and it is likely that we were on the same trip. Small world!

We should be making our way round to Kent this evening for our next pick up. The weather is so rough however that Kevin decides to wait and see what tomorrow brings, so after another tidy up I leave for home.

Our first month and indeed the first part of our season is now over. We are now due a break from school trips, as it is time for the first of the trips to Kent for a week with the "Odyssey" sponsored groups. These trips designed to help rehabilitate cancer sufferers will be dealt with in more detail later.

Peter and I spend the early morning of the first Saturday of May wondering what is happening today.

The weather is better than last night but still not good. For some reason he is reluctant for me to go. Eventually I get a phone call from Kevin saying that the weather has improved sufficiently for us to make a start for Kent on the afternoon tide.

I should perhaps explain here that the group we are working with come through the Chaucer hospital in Canterbury. These are all people who have had cancer and are now in remission. The week's activities, of which we are only a part, include Abseiling, Orienteering and Gliding. They are organised by the Odyssey Trust. On their trips they look after themselves, including doing their own cooking as part of the "adventure and to help them regain full self-reliance.

We cast off at 1315 and make our way down river towards Pyefleet. On the way we pass Tollesbury where Peter is watching our progress from the recreation ground. We chat on mobile phones and Roger and Kevin tease him about what he will be cooking himself for dinner this weekend as compared to what I will be cooking them!

Sunday

During the early hours of Sunday morning the wind gets rough once more and I doubt if we will be able to make our way down to Kent after all. For while *Thalatta* would undoubtedly make the trip, she is nearly one hundred years old and we like to treat her with due respect! By the time I finish making breakfast the weather has improved and while I am washing up Kevin pokes his head into the galley and says "Its OK, we are going to up anchor and get under way".

We have lovely conditions for our trip down, making our way mostly under sail, down across the Thames Estuary to foreign waters, Kent! We anchor off Faversham at about 1430. Roger and Kevin then go ashore in the two boats and return with the luggage for the group we are collecting today.

I wait on board while the boys go back to collect the people. I help everyone on board and then watch as Kevin announces,

"OK people, I've got news for you. This is home for the next few days!"

This comes as quite a surprise to them as they all thought they were just coming out to have a look round the barge!

Kevin, Roger and I are invited to join the group for dinner tonight, which they have prepared themselves. We agree of course and spend the meal satisfying as much of our guests' curiosity as possible.

After dinner I ring Peter and find that he has spent the afternoon in casualty as his legs have decided to go on strike. Twit!

Monday

It is Monday morning and I am unwell and spend most of the day in my bunk! I had better add that it is not food poisoning and has nothing to do with last night's meal. I am told that at some stage we run aground and have three seals watching our efforts to get ourselves clear.

I climb out of my bunk in the afternoon as we sail round the Isle of Sheppey and Queenborough where we see the *"Ross Revenge"*, home of Radio Caroline, anchored. The ship, although still owned by the Caroline organisation and used for recording satellite broadcasts until recently, is now beginning to resemble a rusty bucket and we wonder how much longer she will be around. We anchor in one of the creeks nearby for the night.

Tuesday

It is a pleasant day in early May and I can take

more interest in shipboard proceedings today.

After breakfast the group are prepared to walk out on the bowsprit. There are two permanent lines, part of the standing rigging, which run either side of the bowsprit. The routine is to shuffle sideways along these whilst leaning slightly over and hanging onto the bowsprit itself. This is not nearly as precarious as it sounds especially as Roger is on the opposite side. Everyone has, in any case, a safety harness on. It's not done to lose paying customers!

It is my job to film the proceedings. I have to admire some of the ladies as, although they are really quite scared they do the walk anyway, and afterwards feel justifiably proud of themselves!

Bowsprit walking takes about an hour, after which it is time to scrub the deck. This gives me the opportunity to spray Kevin with the hose. Most satisfactory!

Our next job is to up anchor and head for Gillingham for all the passengers to disembark. Everyone has said their reluctant goodbyes and departed by 1330.

After our lunch we set out for Essex once more arriving at Bradwell at about 2200. Kevin, Roger and I make our way ashore and camp in the local pub, from where Peter is instructed to collect me. Our lines of communication are as good as ever and he goes to one part of Bradwell whilst we are in another.

Some time in the bar restores domestic harmony once more and we leave for home. It is cold and the three of us race to the car. Unfortunately Peter's back problem, which was the reason for his sudden departure to casualty, leaves him running like a ruptured crab and the rest of us collapse with laughter! Fortunately he sees the funny side of it. Roger and Kevin are returned to the shoreline where

View Over The Stern

Approaching The Orwell Bridge

Roger Ready For Anything

Action Stations, The "Battle of Felixstowe"

they have left the barge boat, and Peter and I return home. All in all an evening for which my husband will be teased unmercifully for the rest of the summer.

I now have a few days off.

Scrubbing The Decks

Chapter Eight

Magic String and a firing party!

Monday morning, and Kevin is already on board when I arrive. He greets me with a cheerful "Goin' to make a brew then, Rita?" before he helps me to load the provisions. After a slight problem getting the gas fridge to light we are all ready to welcome this week's group which is from the Fitzwimarc School.

We are under way at 0900 and make our way down river, anchoring off Bradwell for lunch. Today the weather is miserable, even the old power station looks grey and lonely. We have had a thunderstorm and plenty of rain, there are leaks from the skylights into the main hold, so we are beginning to feel damp. I'm starting to feel fed up not even being Third Hand on a barge is fun *all* the time!

After lunch it is up anchor again and we make our way towards Brightlingsea and the River Colne. Despite everything the Group members seem to be enjoying themselves, which is the main thing. They have been up on deck scrubbing, raising and lowering the sails and steering the barge.

We anchor before dinner after which, Kevin gives his talk on filling in the logs and I demonstrate how to get into and out of the hammocks. It is also a good evening for rope tricks. The most often demonstrated of these being "Magic String." This works as follows;

A length of string is held between the thumb and forefinger of each hand. Now the object of the exercise is to tie a knot in the string without letting go. This involves great skill and dexterity as the string has to be folded over the forearm in a particular way, if, with the twist of the wrists, the hands are to be outstretched, triumphantly displaying firmly gripped string and a perfectly formed knot, somewhere near the middle.

When the trick has been demonstrated once or twice by the crew each child is invited to have a go. When they have all failed, Roger takes them through the trick again slowly, step by step. The process is then repeated. However it is seldom, if ever, that anyone is successful, although it keeps them amused, often for hours, and sometimes for a complete trip! This lack of success does not indicate any unusual shortage of skill on the part of our young crews for this is a Sailorman's trick which cannot readily be learned by the uninitiated or revealed in these pages!

Tuesday

Everybody up early on Tuesday, our first full day, and tuck into a full English breakfast. We are more cheerful this morning as the weather is a mixture with sunshine, cloud and wind but at least it's dry. The group starts the day on deck crabbing.

At about 1100 I make a hot drink for two of the boys, leaving them below while I pop up on deck for a moment. When I return below I find them munching on stolen biscuits!

Now it is a strict rule on board that no one is allowed to take anything from the galley without asking. Not even the Skipper would think of doing such a thing as our supplies have to be made to last all week. In the event of bad weather such petty theft could mean people going hungry by the end of the week.

The boys are told that they are in deep trouble and that the punishment will be both fitting and severe! They are to face the firing squad at noon!

At the appointed hour the boys are duly lead up on deck in some trepidation. Here their fellow students blindfold them and tie them to the mast. A suitable squad is then assembled, comprising Roger and me. From somewhere a voice rings out;

"Firing party ready?"- Of course we are!

"Take aim."

"Fire."

At once a salvo of water shoots forth from our weapons, large water pistols we have hidden on deck in readiness. Having been ceremonially "shot" with these large water guns our criminals are duly remorseful, not to say, wet! Everyone finds this great fun and highly amusing. Even the boys themselves see the funny side of things though hopefully learning something of a lesson as well.

After lunch everyone goes off to Brightlingsea. I remain behind and watch as a small grey cumulus cloud builds into a very large black cloud indeed! Suddenly the decks are swept by a thunderstorm, high winds, torrential rain and hail!

The hatch is far too heavy for me to close by myself so some of the wet finds its way down below. We will have to mop it up later but there is nothing that I can do on my own now.

Faster than it arrived, the storm passes leaving me to go up on deck and amuse myself making slush balls out of the hail left on deck. And this is mid-May! It has melted by the time any one comes back to throw it at.

Tonight after dinner, all and sundry go crabbing again but nothing is produced which we can eat!

Wednesday

The weather has changed for the better today, being sunny and warm, though quite breezy. This we take advantage of and make our way to Pyefleet under sail. After lunch the weather deteriorates and we have more thunderstorms with hailstones. It's even too miserable for the youngsters who busy themselves below completing their Log sheets. Kevin and Roger take the opportunity to have a wash and spruce-up. About time too!

Around 1500 the weather has cleared enough for all the children to go ashore on Mersea Stone. Roger takes his fork and Kevin's waders to go and dig worms for bait. After dinner the bait is put to use (notice I didn't say "good use") for crabbing and fishing, although the total catch is only one eel and several crabs. The water is now looking absolutely beautiful with hardly a ripple in sight. An idyllic May evening afloat.

Thursday

A beautiful morning with the river still like the proverbial millpond. As we motor out of the Colne we catch just enough breeze to allow us to set foresail, mainsail and topsail.

While the sails are being set I notice that our water tanks need changing. We have two; one situated under the *shelf,* or Fourth Hand's bunk and one under Rogers's bed. Since we have not yet used enough water to have run either out, this means that we have a problem somewhere! I ask Roger to check the water supply for me. Eventually he emerges from down below with the news that the water pump needs changing.

Annoying as it is to have to do the job at the moment, there is no option but to change the pump. Unfortunate as this is for the boys, we cannot afford to run out of drinking water and what we have in the tanks is all we can get until we are moored somewhere we can connect to a hose to replenish them. Water, like food, is very carefully used on a voyage.

I busy myself elsewhere while the boys carry out

their onerous chore which, in fairness, they do reasonably speedily and with commendable self-control. It was at least a clean job, unlike changing a bilge pump, which would have meant fishing around in a foot or so of filthy water!

In the afternoon Kevin and Roger decided to do some trawling, as Kevin has been given a trawl net comprising a metal frame with netting attached. This is lowered over the side of the barge and dragged through the water. Unfortunately (?) the barge is going too fast and the net keeps rising off the bottom. The resulting haul is one starfish and a jellyfish.

While we were making our leisurely way at 2 knots or so, Roger calls "Here, come and look at this, Rita". Dutifully I respond and am rewarded by the sight of hundreds of purple coloured jellyfish.

Roger warns me "When you see those, Rita, be careful, they are the ones that can give you a very nasty sting". He needn't worry. Since I don't swim, there is little likelihood of me touching any jellyfish unless I fall overboard! Suddenly a voice next to me chirps up, "Wow! I've never seen so many jellyfish in one place in all my life!" It's the teacher, also a Rita, who has come over and is staring in amazement at our escort.

The possible danger from the jellyfish is indeed real. Less so perhaps is the assurance that Roger is likely to give when asked if there are any sharks in the local waters. Sagely he will reply that, apart from small and harmless dogfish occasionally caught, there are definitely NO sharks! After a brief pause for effect he will then equally seriously inform his questioner that this is because the crocodiles have eaten them all!

After dinner we drop anchor off Osea Island, a private Island in the River Blackwater and everyone goes off in the boats except Rita, the teacher, as she has some work to catch up on, and myself. I ring Peter, have a read and thoroughly relax.

Friday

Going home day so its final packing, boxes tidy, hold swept and all ship-shape by the time we tie up in Maldon at midday. Last goodbyes said, it's off home and ready for the British Legion this evening, and a week off. Next week is a "Barge free week", which is our version of a holiday.

Monday

It is now the first Monday in June and we greet St. Christopher's school, a special school from Leigh-on-Sea. Peter has just come out of hospital where he has been avoiding work for a week and is not yet fit for Tesco's duty. My friend Gwen therefore picks me up this morning and we do the shopping on the way to the barge. Kevin and Roger are there when we arrive and help us load.

While we are preparing to cast off we discover that the starter motor for our big diesel will not work. Disaster! This means that we have to remain in Maldon until our engineer, Mo, can get here to sort out what is wrong. We have now to hope that not only can Mo get here today but also that he finds that whatever is wrong is either fixable or replaceable. If not we will have to cancel a voyage for the first time ever!

While we are waiting Kevin and Roger take the group out in the boats for a couple of hours. I remain behind to make an apple crumble.

When the dinghies return there is a water fight in progress. I, armed with buckets and water bombs, join in from the barge. This proves to be a decisive vantage point and I think I am on the winning (or at least dry) side.

It is about 2000 when Mo arrives and we wait

anxiously while he disappears into the mysterious (to me) inner sanctum of the engine room. Much to our relief, he eventually emerges with a grin on his face and the comment that:

"You are in luck, the coil to the starter motor had burned out." While we are wondering how this is lucky, he adds, "And I happened to have a spare one with me so you are all ready to go now!"

Much relieved we are early to bed tonight as Kevin and Roger will be up so that we are motoring at the ungodly hour of 0230 to catch the tide.

Tuesday

I wake up to find we are anchored off Bradwell. After breakfast we motor sedately up to Pennyhole Bay, which guards the Walton Backwaters, a lagoon behind Walton-on-the-Naze where you can find all sorts of treasures, including an island that holds a stud farm and is accessible by a mile long causeway at low tide, and another that is home to an explosives factory. We anchor and Kevin takes the group ashore to play on the empty beach while Roger and I remain on board.

The kids all return wet through and covered in sand having had a great time. Roger rigs up a washing line and we hose down wellies, jeans and tops, much to everybody's further delight.

Wednesday

I once more wake up to a beautiful morning with the sea flat calm. We all enjoy the trip from Walton Backwaters around Harwich and up the Stour estuary to Mistley where we tie up at the quayside at about 1200. Roger takes most of the group ashore to play. Sadly, one of the girls, Kerry has to remain behind with me as she is not well. Looking after youngsters who are "under the weather" is all part of my job and I think I succeed in keeping her reasonably cheerful while the others are away.

About 1330 Kevin goes and collects everyone and brings them back for lunch. Then it is a case of "away we go" once more and we start motoring towards Harwich and Felixstowe. The beautiful weather of the morning has changed to blustery showers which get progressively worse, until Kevin decides that the best thing to do is to drop anchor, this time in Copperas Bay. (Here incidentally, Roger digs up a set of antlers two years later whilst digging for bait.)

By the late afternoon the weather has, of course, changed again and it is gloriously hot and sunny, so it is all hands on deck and no skulking below! Everyone spends their time either playing cards, cleaning the brass, reading or fishing, according to taste.

Our fishermen are on form today with both Kevin and Roger catching sea bass, small and large respectively.

Thursday

We sailed this morning taking full advantage of the tide, motoring leisurely down the beautiful Stour to the sea. We anchor for the night off Osea Island ready to make our way into Maldon as early as possible in the morning.

Friday

We drop the children off in the morning at the end of a quiet but pleasant week, which almost did not happen. I take my leave of the others and make my way home. Kevin and Roger take *Thalatta* up to Woolverstone ready for next week's day sails.

73

The 'Tall Ship' Thalatta, 2nd From Right,
Which Gave Our Barge Its Name (E.C.S.T)

Chapter Nine

Day sails.

This week is dedicated to Day trips from Woolverstone. These day sails are a good part of the season as, together with subscriptions to our support organization, "Friends of the Thalatta", they provide a substantial part of the annual revenue for the Trust.

Peter is still off work and accompanies me on four of the days. These are his impressions of those outings: (*Peter's note: The following is my précis of all four days. Each followed a similar pattern but details obviously varied with wind and tide conditions.*)

The day officially starts at 0730 when we pick up the day's provisions from the Masonic Hall in Tollesbury. For Day sails the meals are not prepared on board as they would be on a normal week but are supplied by an outside caterer, an arrangement which gives Rita a different working week.

We aim to arrive at Woolverstone Marina at about 0900 where the fist job is to load the boxes of food onto one of the large carts and wheel it the hundred yards or so down and across the pontoons to where the *Thalatta* is moored.

Once on board we stow the various dishes in and around the Galley whilst hopefully having time to make Kevin and Roger an early brew. This is also a good time to tease Roger about last nights fishing success or otherwise! By now it is time to have the big kettles boiling and mugs prepared for a welcoming tea or coffee for our guests when they arrive for 1000.

Joe Brannigan, the East Coast Sail Trust Chairman, greets the guests and sees them seated around the large wooden dining table in the hold where Rita and I serve them their drinks while Kevin gives them the safety briefing. This is mainly concerned with how to use the life jackets and advise of the Danger areas on Deck.

Whilst for many of our passengers this will be a reaffirmation of previous knowledge, it never hurts to refresh peoples' memories as, in their freighting days, more than one barge lost a mate overboard when caught by a gybing sail. A graphic description of such a tragedy can be read, by the way, in "Mistleyman's Log" by A H Horlock.

When the briefing is over, it's time to make our way out of the marina complex with its 200 or so deepwater berths, and housing the Royal Harwich Yacht Club, and head down river. As there is little wind we use the big Kelvin diesel engine for the first part of the journey. As we go, we pass the privately-owned building known as "Cat house" built in 1793 and famous for the shape of a white cat placed in a window by day to warn smugglers of the possible presence of Revenue Men. By night it is said, a lantern was used instead.

Within minutes we are sailing between two schools and not of fish. On our right is the magnificent vista of the Ipswich High School for Girls looking down on us from the south bank of the Orwell. Earlier in the summer, Rita and I had attended the wedding reception of last year's skipper Cyril in this grand old building, which began life as Woolverstone Hall in 1776. Among its owners was Lord Nuffield just before the Second World War. The Royal Artillery occupied it during that conflict and it is said that the Navy practiced for the Normandy landings on its waterfront. More recently the building held the London Nautical School and now, of course, the girls from Ipswich.

A moment or so later, we see the elegant Orwell Park School, once the home of Admiral Edward Vernon, famed for the wearing a coat of Gros-grain yarn, called *Grogram,* giving rise to his nickname of *"Old Grog".* Since Admiral Vernon was notorious for watering his sailor's rum they called it after him *Grog.* Orwell Park also played its part in the preparations for the D-day landings as part of the Eighth Army. The "Desert Rats" were here in 1944.

By now everyone is up on deck enjoying the views and the atmosphere of a sedate cruise, and of being the centre of attention for most of the people on the numerous small pleasure craft flitting backwards and forwards around us. We pass Pin Mill, once a smugglers' haven, now renowned for its pleasure sailing and as the home of the 17th Century "Butt and Oyster" Pub. This building starred in TV's Lovejoy series and in Arthur Ransome's children's book, *We Didn't Mean to Go to Sea*. Apparently there is a copy of this book still to be found in the bar. Rita and I wash up and prepare everything for the 1100 tea and biscuits. This done we squeeze in some time up on deck ourselves.

Soon however, I find myself at the stern and Kevin asks, "Do you want a go on the wheel then, Pete?"

"Of course," I reply, "but don't disappear; I've never done this before". Motoring along at 6 knots steering is surprisingly easy, the wheel being very responsive and the course easy to follow. Steering under sail or with little headway is a different matter and only those of our guests with some sailing experience are likely to take a turn then!

We make our way out towards Felixstowe docks, keeping to the right-hand side of the deep-water channel for most of the way. In seafaring, unlike on the roads, we "drive" on the right. Power should always give way to sail. However both these rules have to be applied with an eye to the practical. Small sailing boats fly hither and thither around us when they are tacking and as for a Supertanker, with a stopping distance in miles giving way to a sailing barge, don't even think about it! Outside the channel there are many moorings and there are few opportunities to cut corners. Although Thames Barges are reputed to sail "on wet grass" we would not wish to put this tall story to the test!

The ship to shore radio provides a background to our journey, Kevin being able to pick up advanced information on the container ships making their way up and down from Ipswich Dock. We have to be very careful to steer clear of these, as they have neither the room, manoeuverability or I suspect the inclination to avoid us if we got in their way!

We eventually reach the meeting point of the Orwell and Stour rivers at Shotley, where the great mast from *H.M.S. Ganges*, famous for the many display teams of cadets which have learned their skills on it, still dominates the skyline. We make our way round into the Stour. As there is now more of a breeze, it's time to hoist some of the sails and cut the engine for some authentic Barge sailing. It is also nearly lunchtime so Rita and I are down below setting out the meal. We have to make sure that the plates do not slide off the work surface at one point. Otherwise all is steady and sedate.

On deep sea sailing ships, wooden battens or "Fiddles" round the edges of work surfaces or tables would keep the pots and pans in place, usually. We have metal ones on our gas stove but on the stainless steel work surfaces we use damp towels. These are far more useful with the sedate rates of roll usually associated with sailing barges.

The barge is anchored in the Stour at 1230 ready for lunch. We serve this, with wine of course, with everyone seated around the table in the hold. It is now that Rita and I learn that for a while the wind had got up enough for us to have most of the sails up and indulge in some "crashing and thrashing", much to the delight of the more experienced sailors.

Rita and I leave the others to it in the hold and take the opportunity for some fresh air on deck. It is almost unbelievably peaceful lying in the sunshine with the water rippling past. We look out for seals but this week there are only cormorants to be seen fishing.

All too soon it is time for us to go down below to tidy and wash up. Kevin and Roger organise those of our guests not dozing in the hammocks into working off some of their lunch hoisting the sails and upping anchor!

The wind is still strong enough for us to make a decent speed back up towards Felixstowe. As we do, we pass an old light ship, now with a tall radio transmitter mast on her helipad and bearing the name "Radio Mi Amigo", a legacy of an attempt to recreate the golden years of Radio Caroline.

Turning into the Orwell again we have the opportunity to view the massive container ships being loaded at Felixstowe docks. Each day we have been passed by the "*Sapphire*" on her journeys from Ipswich to the Continent. Now although admittedly painted bright blue, I can think of few things less like the gem stone than this ugly iron monstrosity with her cargo of container lorries, etc. (Sorry *Sapphire*, I am sure your crew love you!)

After washing up Rita and I take more time on deck as we make our now leisurely way back up past Shotley, back towards our starting point. Our guests by now are all very clearly enjoying themselves. Indeed, many are regulars who come every year.

Some of the less charitable among us, mainly the sailors, find some gentle amusement from the efforts of a small yacht which has managed to run itself aground. The general consensus is that they will be stuck for five to six hours.

Back down below preparing afternoon tea we notice that the diesel is running again and that we are manoeuvring. At first this of no interest. However, as the manoeuvring becomes more noticeable below, the horrible thought strikes that perhaps somehow we have managed to get ourselves grounded as well. A hasty visit to the deck produces a far more amusing scenario however as we are greeted with the sight of a number of rear ends bending over the side with boathooks and landing nets, while someone in the bow calls out directions to Kevin on the wheel. Someone has lost their cap in the water and there is a full-scale rescue mission in progress! Eventually Kevin gets fed up with playing around and jumps in the dinghy and heroically rescues the offending item himself.

In due course, we serve afternoon tea and cake and we take this up on deck. We are all perching on the hatch enjoying the world going by and graciously acknowledging the envious waves of other passing river users. When the *"Thistle"*, the only "Sprittie" built in Scotland, briefly keeps station with us, this provides a wonderful sight for the occupants of both barges and a magnificent one for anyone watching from the shore.

We eventually reach Woolverstone Marina at our appointed hour of 1600. Instead of mooring facing the way we are going, Kevin gently approaches the pontoon bow first, just allowing the bow to kiss the wood before letting our stern drift round so that we actually moor pointing in the opposite direction to that from which we have come. It sounds simple but to the uninitiated it looks a very skilful manoeuvre indeed.

With 'goodbyes' said thus ends a wonderful day

for all. It only remains for the crew to finish tying and tidying up, and its off back to Tollesbury for Rita and I. Kevin will stay on board and Roger will frighten a few mullet before making his way home just up the road.

Relaxing Day Sail

Chapter Ten

Emergency measures and a history lesson

It is Monday morning in the middle of June and we are back to a normal sailing week.

An all girl group from Woodlands school this week makes a change. They are sure to be boisterous, though we know that the teacher is very experienced and we expect a good week.

Peter drives me up to Woolverstone for our departure and after enjoying the privilege of being able to make Roger, Kevin and me coffee in MY galley makes his escape before the girls arrive.

We make our way off the jetty with our motor and down the Orwell. It is another lovely day to start our week, with clear blue sky and hot sunshine, so we all have lunch up on deck. After a leisurely feast, the wind is fresh enough to allow us to set the sails to make our way down river to Wrabness on the Stour, just upstream from Parkeston Quay. Here we anchor, still in glorious weather in the late afternoon.

Roger goes to dig for worms while I prepare dinner. I assure you that there is absolutely no connection between the two events! By 2200 all the girls are in their hammocks and everyone is settled down after a good but tiring day.

Tuesday

In the morning we set off for Mistley after breakfast where the girls go ashore for an hour and a half. I think most of them were just interested in finding some shops. If they did, then they missed out on seeing the old maltings, now converted to luxury flats, or even visiting Mistley Towers, the remains of a church built by

Robert Adam in 1776. These were the days when Mistley was expecting to become a fashionable spa. For some reason, it never did.

After lunch we up anchor and have a lovely little sail around until we anchor again at 1630. After dinner this evening we spend some time up on deck "enjoying" the sight and sound of a nearby thunderstorm bearing down on us from the Suffolk shore. Somehow the effect of this sort of weather seems completely different out on the river to at home on land. We seem to be able to grasp far more of the magnitude and power of the storm out here than when so much of its effects are masked by houses and trees ashore.

Wednesday

On Wednesday we have breakfast at 0800 and get away by 0930. This morning the weather forecast dominates our actions as Northerly winds of force 5 to 6 are threatened. Kevin decides that we will motor as quickly as possible and anchor in the relative shelter of the Colne estuary between Brightlingsea and Mersea before the gales arrive!

We arrive safely at our anchorage in time for lunch, then Kevin and Roger decide that since the wind has not strengthened too much they will take everyone in the boats to Mersea Stone, one of our regular stop offs, on the east coast of Mersea Island. Here the children and adults come to play, either on the patches of sandy beach or wander further round the sea wall to the Country Park with its acres of grassland. Kevin remains ashore and Roger comes back to the barge.

Only a few minutes after they've come back on board and while I am cooking the dinner, someone rushes into the galley and tells me that Skye, one of the girls, is choking.

Not only is this our first major medical emergency on board, it is potentially of course a very serious one. I go through into the hold where I find a very distressed girl desperately trying to cough up a sweet stuck in her throat.

My first thought is to strike her firmly on the back to try and dislodge the offending sweet. Having tried this twice with no success it was time for more drastic measures. I grab Skye from behind, link my hands under her ribcage and squeeze hard using what is known as the "Abdominal Thrust" technique which I learned in our first aid course in the winter. This technique is not recommended except in an emergency as if carried out too enthusiastically it can break ribs. However I decide that it is better to risk a cracked rib than have our first passenger fatality!

Fortunately for all concerned, after an agonising couple of seconds, out pops the sweet first time. Much to my relief, not to mention Skye's. I was very pleased that my winters study had its value after all!

Poor Skye is quite upset, understandably enough but with all her classmates, Pam, the Head teacher and Kevin in attendance we soon manage to restore her to her normal cheerful self. It has been a worrying few minutes, however, and proves the value of having an extra, trained hand on board.

Roger came down off the deck a while later and wondered what all the fuss was about.

"What's been going on then, Rita?" He enquires.

"Not much," I reply and continue to prepare dinner. Roger wanders off looking slightly bemused, as he often does for some reason, after asking me a question. He'd missed the "excitement" because he was on deck fishing, and actually caught one!

After dinner we get out a birthday cake and all sing happy birthday to Hannah who is eleven today. Skye joins in, proving that her throat and abdomen have both fully recovered.

There is time for some crabbing before Kevin's talk and bed at the end of an eventful day!

Thursday

The morning sees little change in the weather but Kevin and Roger are keen to take the group to Mersea, so it's all aboard the boats, armed with rounders bats and balls, despite the force 5 that is still blowing today. Everyone is back on board for lunch and seems to have had a good time, apart from doing far too much bickering over the rules of rounders.

After lunch the girls go up on deck and Roger attacks them with water balloons. Those that don't burst, the girls throw back down the hatch at him. I laugh a lot. After the "Battle" it is time to calm down and the girls sit down and enjoy a quiz for an hour.

Friday

Breakfast is scheduled for 0800 today. However, whilst I am up at 0700 as usual to prepare it, no one else is awake! Breakfast does eventually take place of course, after which everyone packs their bags and cleans out their boxes, ready to go home.

We up anchor late morning and then set to work scrubbing the deck. Someone asks me to hold the hose (big mistake). In the water fight that follows Roger is again in charge of the water balloons and most people get agreeably wet.

As we motor up the Blackwater we pass the "*Xylonite*" anchored off Osea Island. This is too good an opportunity to miss. Roger gets some water balloons ready and then rigs our main armament, a big elastic catapult. As Kevin motors up slowly to our target I unfurl the "Jolly Roger" and Roger lets fly with the primary weapon, whilst the girls all provide secondary fire with water balloons. All this impressive firepower (or is that waterpower?) is wasted however as we miss!

One of the girls asks Roger how the *"Xylonite"* got its name.

"Well Xylonite was an early form of plastic, like Bakelite".

"What's that?" Our little inquisitor enquires.

"Well, it's the sort of stuff that things that you are used to seeing moulded in plastic, would have been made in when your Grandad was young. Like I said, an early form of plastic", Roger continues manfully. "Xylonite was made in Brantham near Manningtree and used for such things as the stiffening in shirt collars and for ping pong balls. It was developed at Lawford and the raw materials would have been the sort of cargo that the barges would have carried many years ago."

Roger then poses a question of his own.

"When you went to Mistley, did you see a sign for a company called EDME Ltd.?"

"Yes, I did," said the girl, being a bright young thing.

"Well," says Roger, "If you keep a good look out round these parts, you might see a barge called the *"Edme."* I will let you work out the connection for yourself".

With these few words of wisdom our hero retires to his duties.

Chastened from our lack of a decisive victory in the latest of our sea battles, but in fine spirits, we arrive in Maldon at 1545 where we tie up. The girls all have a sing song whilst we make ready to present their certificates at 1700.

Monday

It is now late June and this week we have swapped the girls for the boys of Woodland Preparatory School. We wonder if they will give us as much fun as their schoolmates did last week.

We make our way out of Maldon on the motor going up and out of the Blackwater until we reach the Colne off Brightlingsea, where we anchor. We take the opportunity to put the boys ashore for an hour or so before dinner and they manage to work up quite an appetite exploring the charming town with its links to oyster fishing and boat building.

Roger goes ashore after dinner and will not return until, Thursday. In his place we have Charles, a friend of Rogers who is studying for his Masters Ticket. We get all the boys settled by 2200 and we retire shortly afterwards, except for Kevin who sits up on deck with two boys who will not stop talking. So that makes three of them!

While missing work for the summer Peter makes himself useful for once by researching some "Barge history" for me. I spend some time before sleeping reading his notes. Translated into something approaching English they are as follows:

"It is said that the first of what we know as the "Thames Sailing Barge" to be built in Essex was the *"Experiment"* built for Samuel Horlock at Rettendon in 1791. At first these vessels were open to allow as much cargo as possible to be stowed. When eventually decks were introduced it meant that large hatches had to be built in to permit the (relatively) easy loading and unloading of cargo.

Just as the internal nature of the barges changed so did their external form over the years. As trade

87

changed from being merely by local creeks and rivers to encompassing coastal and cross channel voyages, so evolved the hull shape. The principle remained however of carrying the greatest amount of cargo at the least cost

One of the more noticeable changes has been the adding of a mizzenmast and sail to the rudderpost to give better handling; this was later moved forward when ship's wheels began to replace the tiller.

To increase power, topsail, topmasts and bowsprits were also added. Bow shapes had by this time also evolved from a shovel shape or "Swimmie" bow to the straight shape we recognise today.

Throughout the nineteenth century barges gradually increased in size, with capacities of 50-60 tons being common by 1890.

As related earlier, in many cases either the boom rig was replaced or a "Spritsail" rig was installed from new. Such rigs were far more economical to work needing a crew of two or at most three, as opposed to the five or six on a "boomie". (Where a barge such as "Thalatta" has a spritsail main rig and a conventional mizzen rig, she is colloquially known as a "Mulie" for obvious reasons).

Another change was that as barges increased in size, ships wheels replaced tillers and the Mizzen sails were moved inboard from the rudder post. As related earlier, probably the best (only?) example of this rig to be seen today is on the diminutive "Cygnet", based at Snape Maltings.

The heyday of the barges saw them trading for a wide range of industries-bricks and ballast for building, malt and barley for the brewers and all sorts of grains and beans for the millers, and farmers. In fact, they were used by almost anybody who needed goods transported around the coast and waterways of England.

As with the First World War, World War Two saw the Barges make a valuable contribution to the Merchant marine war effort, suffering numerous casualties in the process. A number (not *"Thalatta"*) even played a valuable part in the Dunkirk evacuation.

The decline in the numbers of operational barges continued after the war. By 1953, it is said that there were only 163 in use and of these only half carried sails; only 36 being sail alone.

There was no one reason for the decline in the barge trade, rather a combination. The coming of the motor powered coaster, the railways, the development of bigger and more efficient lorries and perhaps more importantly, the development of the roads to carry them. Changes in the pattern of industry and the cargoes to be carried all took their toll. Of all the barges built, about forty are reputed to be seaworthy at the present time. None is in trade carrying cargo."

Reading this brief history I feel both lucky and privileged to be a very small part of the barge story and even more glad that some like *"Thalatta"* do just as useful a job as training ships or pleasure craft helping modern generations understand something of barging history.

Tuesday

The anchor is up at 0900 and we set off under sail for Walton-on-the-Naze, but sadly the wind eases and we have to revert to the "Iron Tops'l" to get us into Walton backwaters where we anchor after lunch.

On the way the youngsters are put to work cleaning some of the ships brass, during which sadly I am forced to shoot some of them, although only with my water pistol, as they are being so noisy! Having just

completed an execution I spot something on the beach.
"Oi, you lot, pipe down and look over there"!

I point to the shore. Despite the youngsters' "enthusiasm" we have still managed to see four or five seals sunning themselves on the beach.

Once settled at anchor the boys take everyone ashore for a BarBQ. This will be of marshmallows and an eel caught by one of the Teachers last night. Tempting as this menu sounds, I stay on board and make a cheesecake for this evening's desert.

Wednesday

It's 0800 on Wednesday and the youngsters are beginning to stir already. Are we in for another noisy, boisterous day? The anchor is up by 1000 and we motor up to Harwich where we tie up by Halfpenny Pier, safely out of the deepwater channel and we all go ashore, Kevin and the boys to play, me to do some emergency shopping. We need custard and lemonade.

The first shop I try is in darkness although otherwise appearing open. I eventually master the local dialect sufficiently to establish that this shop is closed for lunch. I therefore move on to the next one, where I am more successful. I trust that there was more life in the town when Christopher Jones, Master of the *"Mayflower "* was born here and when that ship left this port for it's epic journey. For although everyone knows that the *"Mayflower's"* journey began at Plymouth according to the history books, she only called in at that port because of problems with her sailing partner the *"Speedwell."* Indeed, the passengers were actually picked up from Rotherhithe.

While walking back to the shore I catch sight of the unique brick-built lighthouse with a chimney for a coal fire up the side of it. This historic old building is situated in the centre of the town.

90

With everyone back on the barge we cast off from Harwich pier where we have been moored and make our way under sail up the Stour, past Parkeston Quay from where the ferries and passenger ships sail, to Wrabness where we anchor.

I have three boys to help me in the galley today. Unfortunately two of them, were so badly behaved that they were banned from the Galley completely. They were also disciplined by Kevin, who decides that since we cannot keelhaul them (no keel!) they must remain below decks after dinner while the others enjoyed themselves crabbing.

Kevin's log chat at 2100. Bed by 2200. Everyone has had a good day despite the let down of the behaviour in the Galley. "And so to bed", as one time M.P. for Harwich Samuel Pepys wrote many times in his famous diary. Perhaps even more famously nowadays Zebedee used a very similar phrase in "The Magic Roundabout", but I digress!

Thursday

The kids are up early this morning, making a lot of noise by the time I go through to the Galley at 0800. I am pleasantly surprised to find them already laying the table for breakfast. Good lads!

When we up anchor we motor against the tide as far as Parkeston Quay and then are able to set sail once we are in the Orwell. We have a pleasant little sail round until we tie up on a mooring buoy near Pin Mill.

Kevin takes one of the dinghies and drops Charles at Pin Mill, from where he collects Roger who brings a water gun back with him and manages to spray me. His triumph is short lived, however, and I extract suitable revenge with my guns when he is not looking!

Friday
>We deposit our charges at Ipswich Docks as *"Thalatta"* is to be a feature of their "Open Day". Since I am not required, I get a lift home, arriving just in time for a bath and a much deserved trip to the British Legion.

Monday
>It is now the last Monday in June and as *Thalatta* is still moored at Ipswich docks after the Open Day at the weekend I have to meet her there.

Peter comes with me to "help" with the shopping at Tesco's on the way. This is a disaster as we are in a rush and cannot find the things we need in the enormous Ipswich store. It therefore takes nearly twice as long as usual, added to which we were held up in traffic on the way. It is also pouring with rain.

By the time we finally arrive at the *Thalatta* the school children, from the Appelton School of Benfleet, are already on board and Kevin is starting to look decidedly worried. Although he greets us with a nonchalant "Hi, Rita, get held up?" I can see that he did not like the idea of having to make a choice between sailing without provisions and cook, or missing the tide.

Once Peter has been rewarded with a cup of tea we throw him off so we are able to set out, making our way through the lock and out under the Orwell Bridge. This bridge is always an impressive sight, at least from the water, with its modernistic looking construction and its 128 feet clearance of the water at *high* tide. We motor until we reach the Stour then we raise the sails to cruise up to Wrabness where we anchor for the night.

It rains for most of the day although none of the youngsters seem to mind all that much, being quite excited. Roger has a late dinner as he is off digging worms! The children seem a bit noisy this trip and are still awake at midnight, claiming to have seen a mouse!

92

Strangely enough, no one has ever seen a mouse on board before or indeed since. I am in any case sure that had there been one Roger would have found a way to catch it and use it as bait for something or other! By 0030 I have had enough of excuses and diversions and start confiscating torches. All is soon quiet and sleep prevails.

Tuesday

I wake at about 0630 still feeling quite tired from last night's mythical mouse hunt. I get up at 0745 to find that Roger has made a "brew". Unfortunately the milk is "off" and it is "Yuk!" I make another "brew" just as Kevin comes down cursing about the noise last night.

At 0800 someone accidentally sets off the fire alarm and everyone has to be up on deck with life jackets on. Most of the children are still in their P.J.s. When all has returned to normal, Kevin speaks to everyone about the amount of noise last night. The teachers seem quite embarrassed and I have a woman to woman word with them separately later on.

We make our way up towards Mistley, eventually anchoring just outside. Kevin and Roger take the children to Manningtree in the boats. Since it rains heavily nearly all morning everyone is wet by the time the boys return just in time for lunch. After which it is anchor up again and we motor across the stretch of water known as the "Rolling Ground" and on towards Hamford Water where we arrive and are anchored in time for dinner. This quiet anchorage in the Walton Backwaters was the setting for another of Arthur Ransome's books for children, *Secret Water*.

Thankfully tonight is a quiet night!

Wednesday

Quiet night and a quiet start to Wednesday morning! I am up and into the hold at 0715 on my way to the Galley to prepare breakfast.

Nearly everyone is asleep in their hammocks when I wish them a "Good morning, its time to get up." No great response. I try the teacher's hammock and find her sleeping like a baby. After a couple of attempts I am rewarded with a sleepy look and the comment, "I have no snooze button". "Neither have I," I reply, and leave it at that.

After our eventual breakfast we up anchor and away. It is a good sailing day and we have a full set out as we make our way along the coast past Walton, Frinton and Clacton to anchor off Mersea Stone around 1430. Everyone goes ashore, I stay behind to prepare dinner and make some Angel Delight as a treat.

When everybody returns at 1730 some of them are soaking wet as they have been swimming in their clothes! No harm done, however, and everyone seems to have enjoyed themselves.

After dinner it is crabbing, Roger manages to catch four fish with the "help" of some of the boys.

Thursday

By 0830 two of Starboard team are laying the table with knives, forks and spoons. The bacon and sausages are cooking and the cereals are out ready for eating. A very efficient start to the day!

After breakfast it's all ashore to Brightlingsea for the morning. The old part of the town still has the rows of terraced houses that once housed the families of the men who made their hard livings, fishing in the winter and crewing luxury yachts or racing during the summer. I, however, know the town more for being the home of Brightlingsea Hockey Club, against which we had many interesting games in my younger days.

Everyone is, of course, back on board in time for

lunch, after which we go round to West Mersea so that the boys can be taken ashore to play on the beach. We drop anchor about 1330 and everyone gets towels and swimming trunks ready. No one will get away with swimming fully clothed today!

I remain behind as usual and they all have a great time swimming and playing on the beach even though the weather is cold, wet and windy. Not that that matters a lot if you are in the sea anyway, I suppose! Even the teacher, Sally, has a good swim. Some of the kids made the mistake of asking to meet Roger's friend "Barry". This they did and got wet. Again.

When they all return they sit round the table doing their logbooks while I fill them full of hot chocolate. While this is going on, Roger fishes catching a crab and two eels. Kevin tidies up his quarters.

Friday

We have our breakfast at 0900. Then it is sleeping bags out of hammocks and packing to be done as we up anchor and make our way past Tollesbury and up the Blackwater.

We anchor at Osea Island for lunch at 1300 A century ago the Island was owned by the brewers Charrington and run as a retreat for alcoholics. It is said that local boatmen made more money running illicit spirits than they did from fishing. Tall stories abound in this area, however.

We make our way up past Northey Island which, like so much of the local coastline is an area of Special Scientific Interest with restricted access and managed by the Essex Naturalists' Trust. Making our way back to the quay we also pass the site of the Battle of Maldon, fought in 991, between the Vikings and Brythnoth, the Earl of Essex. We manage to drop our charges off safely by mid-afternoon and I just have time to quickly rush home, have a shower and collect Peter for our next adventure, which I will leave him to tell you about.

95

Chapter Eleven

Fishing?

The adventure starts on Friday evening at the Queen's Head Public House on Maldon Quay where Rita and I meet up with Kevin and Roger for a quiet drink prior to going on board.

Despite the number of people on the waterside all enjoying a "Quiet drink", the beautiful sunset, soft breeze and majestic barges make for an idyllic atmosphere, one of which I think I shall never tire, regardless of how often I enjoy it.

We board the *Thalatta* fairly early, as we are to cast off at three in the morning. There is some discussion as to how best I can help. Staying out of the way is Rita's suggestion. At that time of day this seems good to me.

Accommodation on the *Thalatta* consists of the Captain's cabin in the stern, next to the engine room, The Mate's cabin is in the Focs'l and will also serve as our eating area while our passengers are on board.

Rita, as Third Hand has a tiny cabin next to the Saloon and I will sleep "on the Shelf". This is a bunk which when not being occupied, serves as a storage area. Hence "Shelf".

For the first two nights I use the leader's cabin, which is just behind Rita's, neat and cosy, but eventually I find I prefer the "Shelf".

Saturday

0300 produces noises of great activity above my head. I decide that I am much more use out of the way and go back to sleep!

Sleep cannot last long however and it is just after 0500 that I stick my head out of the companionway to see what is happening on deck. What is happening is that we are motoring quietly down the Blackwater in the early morning light.

Rita soon emerges also and it is time for a brew.

The first cup of tea (for Rita and I) is most welcome as, whilst it may be wonderfully peaceful and even romantic seeing Tollesbury go by in the early morning light, it is also darned cold. I had only meant to go up and say "Hello" and am thus just wearing shorts and T-shirt!

(O.K. so perhaps it was just me who thought Tollesbury looked "romantic" going by etc. etc. Unanimous opinion, however, was that Bradwell Power Station most definitely did not!)

Shortly after we come out of the Blackwater estuary Kevin asks me if I would like to take the wheel. I do not need asking twice.

Motoring along at 5 knots or so the barge is easy to steer providing you know where to go. This vital piece of information is provided by Kevin and basically consists of "steer for that red (or green) buoy in the distance". This is fine providing you can sort out which particular grey blob on the misty horizon is actually the buoy in question.

All proceeds according to plan until nearing the Thames estuary, one of the red buoys seems to be singularly reluctant to get any closer. This does not at first bother me unduly. Distances can be deceptive and the last green buoy had been slow to arrive, and anyway I had noted the course on the compass and was mainly steering by that.

Compass notwithstanding, even I eventually became slightly disconcerted when we do not seem to make any progress towards the "buoy". It is with mixed feelings that I suddenly see the real buoy emerge from behind the rigging on the port side! The yacht I have been following remains in the distance.

I decide to leave it a couple of days before telling Kevin about this. After all we had arrived in the right place and at least it proved I could steer by the compass! I need not have worried, Kevin had known from the beginning exactly what was going on.

Checking The Sails Are Working

After crossing the Thames Estuary we steer towards and eventually pass one of the World War Two anti aircraft forts, used as a first line of defence against airborne invaders and more recently as the home for a number of early Pirate Radio stations. "Radio City" was the one I remember listening to. (See "The Radio Pirates aboard the Offshore Forts in the Thames Estuary" by F. R. Turner for a full account of their history).

Since their ladders were removed to prevent boarding, these great concrete monuments are useful mainly to attract fish and we see a fishing boat moored to one of the tower legs.

By this time Kevin has been sufficiently "stressed" by my driving and has taken the wheel himself to get us to our first destination, the River Swale, just outside Faversham. He is also stressed by the fact that the slight leak, which we had when we left Essex, appears to have got worse!

By the time we arrive around midday the weather has warmed up and we pass a group of eight seals, including three pups sunning themselves on a sandbank as we move up to our anchorage. The sight of these seals is particularly exciting for me as they are the first that I have seen from the barge and the first time I have seen them swim.

On the water's edge we see a number of egrets. I have never seen these large white heron like birds before in the wild and am suitably impressed. I am even more impressed when Roger points out a flock of gulls chasing a marsh harrier! Seen low over the water with the sun shining on its back as it banks and dives the predator looks more beautiful than deadly.

Once safely anchored just by Oare marshes, Rita produces the sandwiches for lunch and we relax in the afternoon sun for a while. It is not long before the combination of the warm sunshine and early start catch up and I stretch out on the hatch for a doze.

Soon however the sounds of the gentle lapping of the water against our hull and the calling of the seabirds are joined by the sound of banging as Kevin and Roger indulge in some carpentry below. Even this cannot keep me awake for long and I drift back to sleep.

At some stage, someone comes up to reassure me that although they are making a lot of noise and removing large chunks of wood from under my bunk whilst looking for the leak, there is nothing to worry about. I wonder how much barge they would hack out if there were something to worry about!

By mid-afternoon I am awake and enjoying the scenery with Rita. I look up as I hear the distinctive buzz of a Gypsy Major engine, being rewarded as I do so by the sight of a venerable "Tiger Moth" as her pilot circles us at 500 feet straining for a better view. I wonder how many times in their respective heydays biplane and barge had shared such a beautiful afternoon. This is an area with an aeronautical connection in that a ballooning club was formed here many years ago, eventually to develop into Short Brothers, makers of the Felixstowe, Sunderland and Solent flying boats among others. One of the founding members of the club was Lord Brabazon, after whom the Bristol Brabazon was named. A beautiful airliner all but stillborn through politics and the jet engine.

Later, Roger and Kevin have to take the boats up the creek to Oare where they are to meet one of the organisers of the Odyssey group, bringing them back to the barge with supplies. Rita and I go along for the ride and we all arrive on shore about 1640.

I should here mention a little about the people we have sailed down to meet. Odyssey is an organisation based in Kent which, to quote from its web site:

"Draws on the majesty of the environment and on art and music, to help people with cancer combat the emotional and psychological devastation caused by the illness. It uses the stimulation of uncertainty and surprise to help participants aged 18 to 84 rebuild confidence and regain their zest for life."

From my experiences with the groups which have been on board *Thalatta*, they certainly seem to achieve their objectives. To further quote from the web site:

"Odyssey helps them to move beyond a time of introspection and despair, and regain a sense of control of the next stage of their lives. The idea is rooted in a great depth of experience of the use of the outdoors to help individuals of all ages and backgrounds. We firmly believe that time spent in the natural environment has a beneficial effect on people, no matter what their background or experience. We also believe that access should not be limited by financial considerations so sufficient funds are raised to enable us to offer all places at no cost to the participant."

A very eloquent mission statement for a very worthwhile organisation.

Our plan now goes seriously wrong as it is intended to have a quick drink in the Shipwrights' Arms before the boys take Charles, the organizer, back to *Thalatta* to show them round, before returning to drop them off and collect Rita and me. The Shipwrights' Arms is, however, closed until 1800!

Undaunted by this tragedy, Rita and I wait on shore while the boys set off for *Thalatta* with their passenger as planned. Having an hour to wait for our pick up, we set off to investigate the possibilities of civilisation along the towpath.

We walk along the narrow track as fast as we can. We have limited time and considerable thirst. Slowing only to avoid treading on a passing field mouse, our efforts are eventually rewarded as, passing the boatyard and reaching the road, we find ourselves on the outskirts of the village of Oare itself. Here at last we find an open hostelry and just have time for a quick half of shandy in the very friendly atmosphere before making our way back.

It has been arranged that we would meet the dinghies at 1730, so it is a brisk walk back to the creek, much enhanced for me as a flash of blue indicates a kingfisher darting across our path as we go. We arrive at the two concrete steps, which indicate the landing stage, bang on the appointed time. Of course Roger and Kevin have not yet returned with the boats.

We spend a quiet and enjoyable few minutes sitting on the riverbank outside the pub where a hundred years ago or less, the sight of a barge moored nearby would have been anything but unusual to the local inhabitants. At one time the sailing barges plied a regular trade carrying saltpetre and sulphur for the local powder works, and in turn carrying away cargoes of gunpowder from the Oare and Marsh works, or bricks from the Ham brickfields. Nowadays only *Mirosa* still powered by sail alone and based at Faversham is a frequent visitor.

Before long, we first hear and then see the boys as they enter our part of the creek. By the time their passengers are safely unloaded it is Opening time!

It has been a very long and hot day so far and a decision is made to refresh ourselves before returning to *Thalatta*.

The Shipwrights' Arms is a quaint, Old English traditional pub with a large well-kept garden nestling, as you will have gathered, up against the sea wall. We sit outside watching the sparrows, blue tits and inevitable pigeons feeding on the bird tables.

All too soon, after one of their frequent checks on the state of the tide, the boys announce that it is time to make our way back. This we do, motoring gently past the rotting hulks on the water's edge and the hot hikers on the seawall, who cast envious glances in our direction.

Back at the *Thalatta*, Rita and I clamber aboard first, leaving Kevin and Roger to bring on the last of the supplies. Rita goes below and I watch as Kevin leans over the side, reaching down for the boxes of supplies which Roger passes up to him. Now this may sound a simple operation as indeed it often is. On this occasion, however, the boxes had been overloaded, thus setting the scene for some truly "Candid Camera" type action.

The first box is handed up, albeit with some effort, from dinghy to deck. As Roger lifts the second, even heavier one, the laws of physics gradually take over!

Helpless, I watch as Roger strains to lift the box high over his head and towards Kevin on deck whist at the other end Newton's Laws of Motion take effect and there is an equal and opposite reaction causing feet and of course, dinghy to move away from us.

For a brief moment it looks as though the Skipper may be able to get enough of a grip on the box to save the day but the gap between the two boats widens still further and, in slow motion all contact with the vital supplies is lost. With a loud splash and some descriptive commentary from the boys, half the trip's supplies bounces off the side of the barge and into the water!

Much to my amazement, whilst the cardboard boxes quickly disintegrate and disappear, the tin cans and the plastic inner bags of the breakfast cereals float gently down river with the tide. This gives our crew the opportunity to display their most inspired side as, rather than showing panic or despair they calmly collect landing nets and pursue their quarry in the dinghies.

I have by now contained my mirth (probably the safest thing in the circumstances) sufficiently to follow the progress of this twilight fishing expedition through the lens of the barge's video camera.

As the light grows too dim for filming I go below to hinder Rita and relate the adventures above. Before long we are joined by our heroes who have managed probably their best catch of the summer, having rescued just about everything except the flour, most of which is leaving a tell tale white streak down the side of our hull!

There now follows a brief conference as to the best course of action. Since there is no chance to replace the stores and there is no evidence that the tins or hermetically sealed bags had actually been compromised it was decided that ignorance would indeed be bliss and to keep quiet!

After a late dinner we all have an early night, but not before Roger displays the remains of his girlfriend's kite, long lost and forgotten, rediscovered during the carpentry work.

Sunday

This morning sees us up for a late breakfast followed by last minute preparations for our guests' arrival. We move all our cooking necessaries from the main galley to the little one in the Focs'l and all my gear from the Leader's cabin to the "shelf".

Once the brass work on deck is polished, it is then time for the crew to enjoy the sunshine and scenery whilst doing their "Coiled Springs" act. This involves remaining as near motionless as convenient, preferably with a passing resemblance to sleeping but (allegedly!) being ready to spring into action at a moment's notice. Roger and Rita are outstanding at this.

In due course Kevin and Roger uncoil enough to depart in the boats to collect our guests.

The boys return around lunchtime and we go through the routine of them coming alongside and asking if they can come aboard to look over the barge. At this stage of course nobody except the Leader knows that they are going to stay on board or that Kevin and Roger are Captain and Mate.

Rita and I play our parts and invite the "tourists" on board. Once all are seated comfortably on the hatch the secret is revealed. This group is of six ladies (plus Ann the Leader) and they are thrilled to be spending the next two days on board, fortunately!

Everyone goes below and, seated around the large wooden table in the hold, the ladies are given their introduction to the *Thalatta*. This covers, of course, the normal safety issues such as life jackets, fire drills and danger areas.

Daysails From Woolverstone Marina

Chapter Twelve
Coast guard to the rescue

Safety issues having been dealt with Kevin explains some of the history of our barge. Fleshed out a little the story is as follows:

"Having initially been purchased by Horlock's after her launch in 1906, *Thalatta* continued in their service until 22 May 1917 when she was purchased by the Wynfield Shipping Co. Ltd., who in turn sold her on to Herbert John Howlett Body on 29 May 1923.

Whilst in the service of Horlock's, the barge had two narrow escapes. On 10th December 1908 she was struck by a severe storm whilst on her way from Sunderland to London fully loaded. *Thalatta* suffered a split main sail and a broken gaff and had to be towed into Lowestoft. A number of other ships and barges suffered worse damage and some were lost.

On the 15th January 1909, whilst carrying a cargo of maize she was in collision with a steamer in the Thames Estuary and had to be towed to Greenwich.

During the First World War, *Thalatta* was busy doing lightering work in the Thames, although on at least one occasion she ran between Shoreham and Dieppe loaded with pig iron.

In 1917 *Thalatta* received her first engine, a 70 hp two cycle vertical oil engine. This was removed, presumably by her new owners, in 1923.

In the 1920s *Thalatta,* although primarily engaged in the coastal trade, also made many trips across to ports in Belgium, Holland and France

Thalatta found another new owner on 5 August 1933 when she was purchased by R & W Paul's who used her mainly as a motor barge, fitting a Ruston and

Hornsby marine diesel in 1947. This engine served *Thalatta* well until replaced by her present motor, a Kelvin Diesel of 112 hp in 1973.

Records still exist of some of her voyages of this period carrying such diverse cargoes as maize, locust beans, oilcake, fishmeal malt, soya bean meal and wheat. Log entries for the period showing journeys as follows:

Sailed 26.10.51 London to Ipswich 610 qrts wheat from SS *Warkworth* Arrived 27.10.51.

The return journey to London was made empty.

Then: Sailed 3.11.51 London to Felixstowe 655 qrts wheat from SS *Daleby* Arrived 4.11.51.

The return journey to London was again made empty.

Sailed 13.11.51 London to Ipswich 638 qrts barley from SS *Muristan* Arrived 14.11.51.

On 1.1.67 *Thalatta* passed from Paul's to John Arthur Kemp, her Skipper. It was he who, with the encouragement of author Hervey Benham and his wife Barbara from West Mersea, restored the barge to a full Spritsail rig again and initiated her conversion as a school cruise ship, continuing as Master until his death in 1987.

Hervey's daughter, Jane, was Mate on board and gives her name (as does John Kemp) to one of the barge dinghies.

Initially *Thalatta* sailed in her present guise under the flag of "Sailtrust" later to become the present "East Coast Sail Trust".

Although there is no precise record of all the Skippers who have commanded *Thalatta* we do have information on some:

Charles Munn is recorded as having taken her from Grimsby to Paris just after WW I.

Fred Grant, who apparently first went to sea at the

age of sixteen, regularly took the barge on the Shoreham to Dieppe run around this time.

As related, in 1923 *Thalatta* passed into the ownership of Herbert Body who, as owner/master took her on the regular timber and grain run to the continent.

Bob Ruffles had command from 1934 to 1947 and Charlie Webb for a time in the 1950's.

From 1956 to 1960 *Thalatta* is shown as being skippered by Bob Wells.

1965 was the last full year in which *Thalatta* carried cargo commercially. In this year she is recorded as being at sea for a total of ninety seven days carrying cargoes of malt, oilcake, fish meal, barley, potash and soya bean from London to Ipswich, Faversham, Rochford, Colchester and Mistley.

Under the Flag of the East Coast Sail Trust, *Thalatta* has had four regular Skippers since John Kemp;

Desmond Kaliszewski 1987 to 1990. Now Master of the *Cygnet*.

Garry Diddams, now an adviser and valued Trust Committee member, 1991 to 1999.

Cyril Varley, Rita's first Skipper and largely to blame for her coming aboard.

Then of course there is Kevin Finch as previously described.

After this brief history lesson it is time for some of the technical stuff. On this occasion it is Rogers's job to deal with this. Some of the ladies ask questions. Unfortunately, they do not yet know Roger and his sense of humour. I am afraid that there is a strong possibility that to this day one or two think that *Thalatta* has wheels underneath to run up on the mud and that the Keelson holds the drive shaft for the bow thrusters!

108

There is a brief opportunity for everyone to relax and explore the barge before it is time for the ladies to set to work in the galley preparing their evening meal.

Rita prepares the crews meal in the Focs'l galley and we enjoy steak and kidney pie and mash while our guests in the main hold enjoy something rather more "healthy eating".

After washing and tidying up everyone is free to go on deck and enjoy the lovely sunset viewed across the Kent marshes, while Roger tries unsuccessfully to persuade Kevin to play his guitar!

The only thing that has marred the day in any way is the constant banging from a clay pigeon shoot being held near the water's edge!

Monday

Waking at 0530 in the morning I go up on deck with the original intention of answering a call of nature. However as I emerge I see three of our ladies already sitting on the hatch soaking up the dawn sunshine.

Original mission temporarily forgotten, I join the girls as we sit watching the terns wheeling and diving for fish in a river, the surface of which is disturbed only by the gentle rush of the incoming tide.

As a further treat we watch as another barge is towed up the creek by a tug. Unlike us she has no engine of her own and has anchored overnight to wait for her tow, a common enough occurrence when sailing in trading days. This prompts one of our ladies to ask if, before they were routinely fitted with engines, all barges took a tug round with them in case the wind dropped!

After breakfast it is time for the girls to wind up the anchor. This they do under Rogers's direction, four at a time in shifts. The anchor is raised by winding on two

109

large handles at either end of a wooden drum (OK, that's not an accurate technical description but you get the picture, I hope).

It is my job to video the week's highlights for the Trust's records and this is a good start. (Previous "fishing" highlights will not be included!)

Once the anchor is up we are off sailing out of the Swale, round the Isle of Sheppey towards Sheerness. We see more seals and egrets, which continue to fascinate me.

Once everyone has had a brief period to relax and enjoy the sailing, it is time for Anne the leader, to organise the bowsprit walking once we are anchored.

Each of the ladies in turn is fitted with a safety harness, which is attached to one of the ropes running the length of the bowsprit. They then climb over the bow and while holding onto the bowsprit itself walk sideways along ropes until they reach the very end.

Whilst there are a few looks of apprehension beforehand, with Roger walking with them everyone makes it. The looks of triumph on some of the faces when they do their Kate Winslet impressions at the end are deservedly well documented on film and video!

Lunch is sandwiches on deck in the sunshine once more, after which, with a mixture of motor and sail we pass back round the Isle of Sheppey into the Medway.

All our ladies take a turn steering the *Thalatta* under Kevin's *expert* direction, while Roger organises the girls helping with the raising and lowering of the sails as necessary.

By late afternoon we have made our way up past the docks, past Queenborough to our anchorage in Stansgate Creek. Here we stop for the night, with distant views of the big ships and docks on two sides and the more pleasant outlook of marsh and fields on the others.

110

This evening we are invited to join our guests for dinner and for wine. This we do, eventually retiring near midnight.

It is another early morning on deck enjoying the sunrise. Fewer people today and quieter. Perhaps the ladies are being considerate of Kevin who spent all day yesterday teasing them about the amount of noise they were making above his cabin at 0600 or thereabouts!

It is changeover day and as soon as breakfast is over the girls once more raise the anchor so that we can proceed to Gillingham.

We make our way up the Medway, past the Darnet Forts and anchor once more near to the quay at Gillingham. Everyone has enjoyed themselves immensely and Kevin, Roger and Rita are profusely thanked for their efforts.

So much do our ladies seem to have enjoyed their stay that it takes two attempts to get them ashore, someone having left some of their belongings behind!

Rita and I are now left alone for a few minutes while we wait for the new group to arrive. Our first ladies have described their colleagues as "much quieter". That would not be difficult!

We soon meet our new friends, as it is only a short distance between our anchorage and the Gillingham waterfront. This group is of the same size as the first but with Duncan in charge, and one other man, Geoffrey in the party.

All aboard and formalities taken care of, we are able to make preparations to get under way. This group do not all look quite so thrilled to be coming on a barge and I wonder how some of them will settle in. (I need not have worried!)

The group is certainly different in character to

the first, perhaps on average slightly older, and certainly less exuberant.

First our guests have of course to haul up the anchor, and then we raise some sail. By the time they have finished their chores they all seem to be enjoying themselves and to have generally settled in.

We now make our way back out of Gillingham and up the Medway to our previous anchorage at Stansgate.

Duncan is a keen map-reader and he and some of the ladies try to pick out and identify various points on the shore. Duncan is also into health foods and fitness and goes round offering us all nuts, some of which he tells us are bitter! He does not get any takers from the crew.

When we reach Stansgate and drop anchor, I get into conversation with Geoffrey and continue to admire the egrets. While Rita is down below showing the ladies where everything is and how it works in the main galley, Kevin and Roger take the chance for a wash and tidy up.

We are invited to join the group for dinner tonight, which spares Rita cooking. We join our guests and play hunt the meat in the rice! The wine is good, however, and we are regaled with various stories, including some funny ones, from when Geoffrey was flying Dakotas during his days as an airline pilot (he is eighty years young!). He is more reticent of his adventures flying Corsairs in WWII.

Wednesday

Our guests seemed somewhat alarmed last night to learn that they had to be up at 0800 to haul up the anchor! Up anchor it is, however, and we make our way down the Medway once more, bound for Faversham again.

It is another heavenly day with enough of a

'Pudge' Comes Back To Maldon

Tucked Up For The Winter

With Skipper Cyril

Rigging

breeze to make the engine unnecessary and clear blue skies. Everyone takes their turn at the wheel and there are, once more, a lot of very happy looking faces.

As we make our way round the Isle of Sheppey we get another chance to see the wreck of the *"Richard Montgomery"*, a Liberty Boat sunk in 1944 when she was misdirected to too shallow an anchorage and subsequently went aground. Although much of her cargo was taken off before she eventually broke her back, the munitions which remain, make her too dangerous to move or to dive on and she remains a potential hazard to shipping.

Lunch today once more consists of sandwiches, tea and sunshine. As we near our previous anchorage opposite Faversham Creek we are again greeted by the colony of seals, which we saw on Sunday. This time we sail closer and we have a marvellous view of them as they swim out to inspect us.

Once the anchor is down and all secured on board it is time for this group's turn at walking the Bowsprit. Again Roger shepherds everyone out and all make it to the end. More happy snaps and video.

We are again invited to dinner this evening. However, with the bowsprit walking and everyone generally winding down, there is little movement towards the main galley! By about 1900 the Captain and crew are beginning to feel slightly mutinous, not to mention hungry!

After Rita shows superb skills of negotiation, it is agreed that she will cook our meal and that we will take ours through to eat with our guests. As it turns out they are still cooking rice while we tuck into our steak and kidney pudding. All to the sound of Duncan interpreting Simon and Garfunkel on his guitar.

We do however join the others for a glass of wine and the evening passes in a convivial manner, if more restrained than with our previous guests.

Thursday

Thursday morning dawns perhaps the most beautiful of them all. I am up on deck at 0600 and am at a loss for words to describe the scene. Expressions like "Golden sunrise" and "water like a sheet of glass" are hackneyed but none the less true for that.

I sit for a few minutes, call of nature, and Kevin's early morning tea forgotten as I enjoy a scene that it would take a poet laureate (and an exceptionally good one) to do justice to.

The tide is not yet disturbing the smoothness of the water and there is literally not a cloud in the sky. It is already warm enough for clothing to be a matter of protocol rather than necessity.

The terns are again fishing and I watch, as one seems to misjudge its height and splash heavily into the glassy water. (Sorry, another one of those overused expressions.) I wonder just how many airmen have made the same mistake in similar conditions but with more tragic results.

I go below to carry out my original mission but have to encourage those who are awake to go on deck. I don't know how many did, but those who did not missed an experience that comes seldom, if ever, to those of us who are land bound.

Eventually we all have breakfast bacon, sausage and egg for us as usual. I don't know what is served from the other galley.

All too soon packing is done and it is time for farewells. Our guest crew have all enjoyed themselves and Geoffrey has been particularly game, keeping up with the girls and making sure the tables were properly and smartly laid out for all their meals.

It is 1100 or so when we set out from Faversham and Kevin reckons we should get back to Maldon about 2000 which will be just right for the evening tide.

Although it has been a good trip and the reactions of all our guests has been most rewarding, all are now tired and greatly looking forward to getting home.

The Wood Burner

The wind is from the southeast so, in addition to the engine we run with the tops'l up. This allows us to make rather better than the five knots or so we made coming down.

Kevin bravely allows me to take the wheel for the trip back, but wisely does not stray far from my side.

We come out of the Swale and head across the Thames estuary in blazing sunshine, I notice that Rita and Roger are engrossed in one of the barge's bird books. It later transpires that the lucky couple have seen an osprey hunting low across the water.

Kevin takes the wheel to see us across the busy Thames' shipping lanes before I settle down to "driving" again.

By now we are well within sight and sound of the experimental firing ranges at Shoeburyness. Whilst we are all familiar with the sounds of gunfire coming from the ranges, it is a new experience for us to see the smoke rising from the detonations and to see what resemble star shells exploding in the air.

Shortly after passing out of sight of the ranges we spot a "Tall Ship" on the horizon. Kevin thinks from the radio chatter that he has heard that this is the replica of Captain Cooks bark, *"Endeavour"*.

As we come closer we get a fine view of what the National Maritime Museum describe as "The world's best replica of an 18th century ship". She is on her way from Whitby to the Royal Arsenal Pier at Woolwich where she is to spend a few days on display.

After a long, hot wonderful sail we reach the mouth of the Blackwater Estuary. Here we are able to see some of the other Maldon barges plying their trade. Kevin, now back at the wheel has to thread his way past his old barge, the *Reminder* as she tacks her way up river.

In the distance we see a Dutch barge making its way round towards Brightlingsea and later still a very pretty little vessel which I take to be a fishing boat with leeboards. Kevin tells me that this is also a Dutch barge, albeit a small one.

We eventually make it back to Maldon but we have made such good time on the way back that we arrive before the tide. (Thus leading to a certain amount of teasing reference to me having taken a shortcut!)

Ahead of schedule we creep into Maldon Quay with the water and Rita and I depart for home while the boys secure *Thalatta* and head for the pub. This concludes a very enjoyable and calm week.

Although mine was a peaceful and relaxed trip, the next year Rita was to "enjoy" a rather more eventful trip to Kent. This is how she was to relate it to me when we were preparing this manuscript:

"It was on a Chaucer trip with Grant on board as mate, as Roger was taking a much-deserved break somewhere on holiday.

We were anchored in Stansgate Creek off the Kent coast with a force eight wind blowing. Kevin and Grant were up on deck lowering the topmast so as to reduce the amount of rocking from side to side, which we were suffering. The mast can be raised and lowered from deck level in much the same way as the sails and with just as much effort, especially in a high, cold wind! In their trading days not all barges carried a topmast or topsail. Indeed for a time *Thalatta* did not. Barges so rigged were called "Stumpies".

I was down below with our passengers, three men and seven ladies, enjoying a game of "Trivial Pursuit", warm and comfortably out of the way when one of the men started behaving oddly. Hardly had we noticed anything wrong when he suddenly went into a fit. Fortunately on this occasion my first aid skills were not required, as one of the ladies was a qualified nurse. Quickly assessing the situation she got the unfortunate fellow laying down on the ceiling and wrapped in a blanket to keep him warm, calm and comfortable.

Kevin was called from the deck and he immediately used the radio to call up the Coastguard who advised that they would despatch the local lifeboat immediately. After what seemed an age in the rolling sea and high winds, though in fact, in less than half an hour we saw the RNLI vessel approaching and very shortly she was nestled securely alongside.

The first job was of course to get a Paramedic on board to check on the condition of the patient. This was fortunately deemed to be good enough for him to be transferred to the lifeboat and thence to hospital ashore. The lifeboat team skilfully strapped the patient onto a stretcher and very carefully carried him up the companionway to the still very windy deck

Now came the hardest part of the job as with the sea rocking the two vessels back and forth, the swell lifted them up and down and with the wind sweeping across the deck, the stretcher was passed across our quarter boards and onto the waiting rescue boat. Shortly thereafter, much to our relief, the lifeboat departed to the safety of the shore and for our former passenger to the benefits of Maidstone Hospital where, to the best of our knowledge, he made a full recovery.

By this time it was after midnight and all thoughts of board games had been forgotten. I was glad to turn in but some of the ladies enjoyed a further quiet glass of wine before turning in at the end of an eventful evening"

Heading For Kent

Chapter Thirteen
Mystery object and some barnacles

Back to normal Monday to Friday sailings this second week in July, with me, Rita. again in charge of the diary as well as the shopping. As usual at the beginning of the week I arrive with a carload of it.

Our group from Northgate High School is aboard by 1145 and we set out. Today is different to usual as the wind is blowing from the east and therefore directly against us so our engine will not give us sufficient power and steerage to make our own way off the quayside. As we may have done in the days before barges had engines, we wait for a tug to tow us into the river before making our way under motor to Osea Island where we drop anchor and have lunch.

In the afternoon we make our way up to the mouth of the Colne to our anchorage off Mersea Stone, arriving at 1730. Here we settle into our usual evening routine of dinner followed by me demonstrating how to get in and out of the hammocks and Kevin briefing everyone on the use of the logbooks. We then settle down for an early night, much as we have done on many Monday evenings.

Tuesday

After our breakfast at 0800 we find that the wind is in a much more helpful mood today, so we wind up the anchor and hoist the sails! There is a fine breeze and the sun is shining again.

We are able to have a lovely sail down to the River Crouch, passing as we do the flat and, from the sea, apparently featureless Dengie Peninsula, named from the small village at its centre. Leaving Burnham-on-Crouch and it's famed yachting centre behind us to our

119

starboard we make our way up river where we anchor for the day. In the middle of the afternoon. Roger and Kevin take everyone ashore for some shopping and games of rounder's and non-stop cricket.

After dinner Kevin organises the children to hoisting the dinghies onto the davits. This is done with great gusto and considerable energy, as to wind up the weight of even these small boats, requires considerable effort for all but the strongest of youngsters.

Kevin then makes an announcement.

"Right. You are all going to wash your hands for a hand inspection".

There is, at first a look of incomprehension on some of the faces until someone has the temerity to ask,

"Why?"

"Because whoever has got the cleanest hands gets to put the bait in the crab net!"

Now this is considered to be both a great honour and highly amusing and I don't think I have ever seen so many hands washed so quickly!

While the crabbing takes place Roger tries to do some fishing but finds his rods all tangled so asks me to sort them out. This I do. Seeing me in unfamiliar territory - near fishing gear - Kevin tries a wind up.

"Pass us a worm will you, Rita?"

Laughingly, since they all know I hate fish and hence fishing, I reply,

"It would shock you if I did."

"Yep."

"Here you are then."

I pass him a wriggling little darling much to his (and my) surprise.

Roger says he can't believe it. Neither can I! I still can't believe it as I sit and watch a beautiful sunset before going to bed - I must be getting the hang of this barging lark!

Wednesday

Unusually this morning, Kevin decides to get the anchor up before breakfast and he and Roger eat on deck while everyone else has theirs below. After breakfast Roger comes below and tells us that we are all to go on deck, me included. This I do while Roger stays below to do the chores.

On deck, Kevin gets us all to sit quietly on the hatch as we pass the Buxey Buoy. There we watch eleven seals and many cormorants as they play on the riverbank. Although I have seen such things before, I still find that I am fascinated with this view of the world that I could never have from shore. The kids, I am pleased to say, love it, and Rachel, the teacher is "over the moon".

After out "nature watching" we come down to earth and decide to scrub the decks. This is done, not only to keep them clean but also to prevent the wood from drying out too much and cracking. We have a splash around with the hose, with everyone using brooms on the wet decks. When the children's work is done we use the hose to wash their hair, even Kevin coming for a shower. Much refreshed we all dry off by sunning ourselves on the deck!

We set off for Mersea Island and on the way see something unusual floating in the water. We cannot make it out at first even through the binoculars.

Opinions vary as to what the object can be,

"Dead seal?"

"Porpoise?"

"Dolphin?"

"Bomb?"

Imaginations work overtime. There is only one way to find out and Roger is launched in a boat.

Investigation reveals the mystery object to be a dead porpoise, which Roger tries to get aboard to find out how it died. Fortunately however the carcase is too slimy (and smelly) for Roger to get out of the water and it is left behind. On returning to the barge Roger notifies the coastguard, but they are apparently only interested if it washes up on the beach. Not very helpful, but I suppose they have to have their rules like anyone else.

After dinner Kevin and Rachel go ashore to see if there is a lifeguard at the open-air pool. There is! Yippee! All the children are excited at the prospect of going swimming and rush round to get their things ready. Everyone departs about 1415, as they leave, Roger calls out to me to get his fishing rod in.

As the dinghies disappear towards Brightlingsea I dutifully reel in Roger's line. As I do so I feel the weight of something on the hook. As it clears the water I see that I have caught an eel. Both of us are surprised! Not knowing what to do with it if I get it on board I give the rod a wiggle and the eel has the sense to slip off back into the water. I am left wondering who has caught who.

Thursday

While I am cooking breakfast this morning Roger visits the Heads. Shortly afterwards I see one of the boys going up to find Kevin. Apparently one of the pipes has burst all over Roger. Yuk! Roger and Kevin thus have to take the Heads apart and repair them before breakfast, which they, now clean thank goodness, have late.

The weather is not good today, being very gusty. We spend the morning with card games, rope tricks and of course crabbing. Lunch is at 1300 after which, since the weather is still bad, we play table tennis. Roger and I are partners, but for some reason are branded as "Losers" and "Cheats." I can't think why!

Two of our young crew, Stuart and Nathan are on dinner duty today and make pizzas and salad (very nice too).

After dinner the kids do 'word searches' and a quiz until for some reason a massive water fight breaks out on deck! Rachel is on the receiving end of a couple of buckets of water, and water bombs go down Rogers's hatch. Kevin has taken the precaution of wearing his waterproofs.

When the combatants all come below to get ready for bed, they are dripping wet! Roger and myself are damp.

Friday

Everyone is excited at the prospect of returning home but sad to leave the *Thalatta*. Goodbyes said, we all make our ways to our respective weekend retreats. Kevin, no doubt to play with more boats, Roger to enjoy a quiet pint, and me, to be pampered by my husband. Oh look, there goes another flying pig!

Monday

We begin the week with a late start at 1430, as the school, St. Aubyn's from South Woodford, is not due on board until 1630. We are even later getting away as we have to wait for *Hydrogen* to board a party of 48 as we are moored between the Quay and our sister barge, and hence 'imprisoned' until she has cast off! Thus we only have time to make our way to Osea Island before dropping anchor ready for dinner. By the time we have cleared up from the evening feast, there is just time to demonstrate hammocks before everyone is asleep for one of the quietest Monday nights of the season!

Tuesday

We are up promptly this morning ready for an early breakfast. Once fed, it's on deck to up anchor, and we make our way, under sail, to Mersea Stone. We have lunch as we sail and finally drop anchor again a little after 1300. The children are quiet again this morning and go below to write up their logbooks! The quiet is eventually broken when, in the middle of the afternoon I spot a seal eating a fish and hurry below to tell everyone. It is then a mad rush to get up on deck to watch, amid much excitement.

After seal spotting the boys, that's Kevin and Roger, of course, take the children ashore to play cricket and football while I get on with preparing some angel delight for dessert.

They are all back on board by 1730 having apparently having had a great time, except possibly for Roger, who has been stung on the toe by a bee.

Wednesday

Breakfast is nice and early as everyone else is going ashore to Brightlingsea.

Once they have gone I make lunch. Today it will be chicken, sausage, or cheese sandwiches. Once this is done I enjoy some peace and quiet to myself for a change. There is no real privacy on board unless I am shut away in my cabin, so these times to myself are much treasured.

The boats return in time for lunchtime. Whatever they have been doing ashore seems to have woken up the children for when we up anchor, there is the most noise and excitement we have had this week. It may have been learning some of the history of the place, of course; about the swing bridge turning on bearings the size of footballs, or the railway line used for transporting sprats. Somehow I doubt it, however! Whatever the reason, the girls and boys are trying to out do each other for enthusiasm!

We proceed under power to Mayland Spit on the

south side of the Blackwater where we anchor for the night.

Thursday

Kevin and Roger are up early this morning and we wind in the anchor at 0700, motoring to Goldhanger where we anchor once more in time for breakfast. When this is finished the children are taken ashore to play in the park. This has two benefits, firstly it allows them to work off some of their excess energy, and secondly, it allows us to rid ourselves of some unwanted passengers! Over the season we have collected some stowaways in the form of barnacles which have attached themselves to the bottom of our hull. These slow us down and need to be scraped off; a job I am very happy to leave to the experts, Kevin and Roger! This is a job best done at our present position, as once the tide has gone out and *Thalatta* is sitting high and dry (?) on the mud, we have plenty of room around her to do the work.

Once the barnacles have been scraped off, the hull needs to be painted with "anti-foul"; another job best left to the boys! By afternoon brew the painting is finished, and all and sundry are back at the barge. With the hard and dirty work done it is a good time to let off steam and everyone dons boots and plays in the mud, sliding and sprawling until they look like so many seals squirming on the shore. I stand on deck and laugh at their antics.

Before dinner everyone comes back on board, filthy dirty, soaking wet and having had a great time. So it is pizza and salad for dinner, after which it is up anchor and make our way to Osea Island and prepare for an early trip back to Maldon and home in the morning.

Friday

Early start, and finish up logs, present certificates, etc, before home time.

Monday

I arrive on board at the beginning of the last week in July, having done the shopping en route. Young Ben, a lad in his mid-teens who is along as Fourth Hand this week, greets me. This means that he is with us mainly to gain experience of being out on the barge, but also to be a help to me. It is not often we ship an extra crewmember. Usually it will be someone we all know and get on with since they share our living space. Ben is the son of one of the local watermen and thus we know the family.

The group, from St. Cedd's in Chelmsford, arrive just before lunch and we are ready to cast off at mid-day. We have a pleasant motor up to Mersea Stone in the warm sunshine before anchoring for the night.

Tuesday

We have breakfast at 0800. Then we motor up to Hamford Waters in a force 5-6 wind. Everyone sits up on deck. As it was a bit "Roly Poly", no one could walk in a straight line! This is one of the few occasions when the weather actually makes many people uncomfortable, as a barge is a very stable craft and it is usually quite difficult for me to notice much movement when I am working down below. We are very glad when it settles down for the youngsters in the afternoon.

We finally arrive at 1700 and drop anchor in the sheltered backwaters. We get dinner organised, after which we have plenty of time for crabbing, which Ben joins in enthusiastically, before lights out at 2200.

Wednesday

As we make our way out across the "Rolling Ground" we are lucky enough to again see the bark *"Endeavour"* making her way from Harwich up to the River Orwell on a day trip. As ever the sight impresses us.

We make our way towards "The Bar", a nasty

126

sandbank, which is at the mouth of the River Deben. The channel is not very wide here and, channelling as it does some ten miles of waterway, can lead to some treacherous currents, we are careful to keep to the middle. All safely negotiated we drop anchor in time for lunch of sandwiches and cake.

After lunch the boys take everyone ashore in the boats to Felixstoweferry, the hamlet opposite Bawdsey, to see the ferries and to have a walk along the sea wall. Whilst they are ashore the heavens open and everyone looks like getting soaked, Ben and the teachers included. However, Roger takes all the kids into a cafe for a cup of tea while Kevin heroically comes back to the barge for the waterproofs. Thus, despite the thunderstorm, he is the only one to get wet!

After dinner the adults enjoyed the beautiful sunset. So perhaps the sun does shine on the righteous, after all! The children were only interested in crabbing! Roger however tells me the story of the Manor House in Bawdsey, built by a stockbroker by the name of Quilter in 1886. He is said to have built one tower for each of the millions he made. The nine towered building was taken over by the government in 1936, and Sir Robert Watson-Watt and his team did much of the work there which kept us a vital nose ahead of the Germans in the development of Radio Direction Finding, or *Radar* as we now know it. Husband Peter will be interested in this story as even he manages to get enthusiastic when learning that the Marconi Tower in Baddow is one of the original Chain Home masts used in the Battle of Britain!

Thursday

After breakfast we up anchor and move along the river to a local beauty spot known as "The Rocks". Here there is a beach with fossils to hunt and trees with ropes on so that the more adventurous can play "Tarzan" (and

"Jane"). Later Kevin, Roger and the group go into Woodbridge with a picnic lunch while I stay on board and make jellies for dessert tonight.

Dinner is at 1830 after which everyone gets packed ready for an early departure tomorrow. We are not, however, at our normal berth in Maldon but will be staying at Woodbridge to be one of the attractions at their

Regatta weekend. From where we tie up at the quayside we can see a tallish white, timber-clad building on the waterfront. This is the Tide Mill, built in 1793 but much restored. There has been a Tide Mill on this site since Roman times and it is now one of only two left in the country. The other is at Elin, near Southampton. This

Souvenir Shop In The Saloon

building is a major attraction for Woodbridge though the town's greatest claim to fame is the ancient ship burial site at nearby Sutton Hoo; and, of course, its annual regatta!

Friday

Goodbyes are said and departures made by lunchtime. Peter collects me in the early afternoon and we leave *Thalatta* behind to enjoy her open days over the weekend. Ben has enjoyed himself no end as Fourth Hand, joining in with the kids and helping Kevin. He stays behind in the afternoon to help the boys dress the barge with flags ready for the festivities.

128

The Main Horse And Crab Winch

At Anchor Near Aldeburgh

Wining And Dining, The Table Set For Daysails

Chapter Fourteen

Mutiny

We start August with another group from St. Cedd's school. It is a late tide today so it is 1630 before we get a tow off the Woodbridge Quayside by Tam, or at least his tug!

Gemma, an attractive blond in her late teens, is on board as Fourth Hand this week. Perhaps it is a good job that this week's group will not include any teenage boys! Because we have had to leave so late we can only get as far as "The Rocks" before anchoring for the night.

Tuesday

A very hot day again today by the looks of things! Definitely a day to be out on the river rather than slaving away indoors somewhere. We make our way up to the Felixstowe ferry port. where we anchor for a while and enjoy the view, before moving off again, "punching the tide" as we call it; that is, motoring against the flow. We make our way out of the River Deben, having lunch on the move, and everybody takes the chance to "top up the tans".

We eventually anchor at Hamford Waters in time for dinner after which there is plenty of opportunity to enjoy the traditional evening crabbing. I relax in my cabin and don't notice if my Fourth Hand is helping with this.

Wednesday

Today is forecast to be the hottest recorded, although in the end it falls short by a couple of degrees F. Breakfast at 0800 after which everyone else goes ashore to play on the beach. I am boring and stay on board to make cheesecake for dessert.

Even in today's temperature all manage to tear themselves away from the beach in time to get back on board for lunch at 1300, after which we up anchor and make our way towards Brightlingsea. It is now very hot indeed and the sea breeze is doubly welcome, as it allows us to sail rather than using the motor and cools everyone up on deck but not much!

As I take my chance to relax on deck for a little while making the best of the conditions I reflect that work can be very pleasant at times. I am laying on the hatch looking up at the sky when one of the children makes a comment about the fact that I am sunbathing and not working. I very seriously inform them that I am doing the vital job of checking that the sails are working properly!

I never know if I am believed or not. What is for sure, however, is that my job as Third Hand nowadays differs in many respects from the one outlined by "Chubb" Horlock in the book "Mistleyman's Log".

Speaking of the early part of the 20th Century Chubb relates how the Third Hand was, in addition to being the cook, the general "dogsbody" of the barge (nothing changed there then!). Responsible for such menial tasks as ensuring that all the ship's brass is kept polished, cabins are scrubbed out and general cleaning. Come to think of it perhaps not that much has changed at all!

Jobs I do not have to do now, however, unlike my predecessors are filling the water tanks. That and lighting the coal fire so that we can have breakfast is a job for Kevin and Roger. We have a slightly more modern gas stove nowadays.

One job I definitely do not do which fell to the Third Hand in the First World War (and probably the Second) is that of standing in the bows watching out for mines!

As soon as we anchor at Mersea Stone everyone goes ashore on the deserted end of the Island again for more swimming. I stay behind and cook, both the dinner and myself in the Galley.

Thursday

I am the only one awake at 0700 and I make Roger jump when I take him in his coffee. Gemma, my helper, is still sound asleep on the shelf! Breakfast is served at 0800, after which the youngsters are taken ashore to do some shopping in Brightlingsea. Kevin comes straight back to work on the generator, which refused to run last night! I display my great technical ability by holding the torch. Despite our combined efforts the generator stoically continues to refuse to work. Although we can cope without it, we will be restricted to our back up 12-volt system until someone fixes the generator at the weekend.

Our shoppers are back on board by 1230 for lunch on deck in boiling sunshine. After lunch it is up anchor and off to Osea island where everyone goes off to play on the beach again. Roger stays behind to paint the deck and I prepare dinner. Early meal this evening, 1815, after which the children pack their cases before settling down to some serious crabbing.

Roger has a good evening's fishing and catches two sea bass.

Friday

Everybody is off early in the morning. Once everything is clean and tidy for next week the crew are also off for an early home time.

Monday

I leave home at 0900 and stop at Tesco's for the remainder of the shopping. Sharron (my elder daughter) is with me and helps load all the provisions aboard when we arrive. I suspect this is as near as we will ever come to getting her on the barge.

Shortly after Sharron and I have finished our provisioning, the week's group, our third from the St. Cedd's School in Chelmsford comes on board at around 1045. Joe, our chairman shows the parents around the barge and gives them a brief history lesson.

We leave the quay with the tide at mid-day and make our way to Brightlingsea where we anchor for the night. Roger and I remember the time we decided to "ambush" our Skipper here.

Kevin had been taking the rubbish ashore to Brightlingsea in one of the boats. It was a nice warm sunny day so we decided to give him a nice cool surprise when he came back.

Roger prepared the water bombs and loaded the super soakers while I laid them out on deck in readiness. The children were then carefully briefed to carry on crabbing as the dinghy was seen approaching our barge. I went below deck, as did Roger as Kev neared the barge. Despite some rather suspicious giggling, the kids managed to achieve complete surprise, bombarding the unsuspecting Skipper with the full armoury of water weapons, including some buckets of water from the pump.

Eventually our "mutineers" relented and let Kev on board to get changed. Once dried out Kevin managed to see the funny side of things, which was just as well. Roger, and I had not been able to keep straight faces any longer.

Tuesday

We motor as far as Walton Backwaters and then get all the sails up. After an enjoyable sail round we anchor at 1430 so that we can go to the beach, (me included!). This is a real treat, as our little spot is always quiet as it cannot be reached from the land and very few people know of its

132

existence. Kevin and the kids have a swim, Roger digs for bait and I take a stroll along the shore for about 30 minutes.

When I get back Roger and Nick, one of the leaders, are sitting on the side of the dinghy, while Kevin is scrubbing its bottom. I go for a paddle and then sit on the dinghy to add my weight to the side. My feet are in the water and my bottom in the dinghy. This is fine until I came to get up, then I find I am stuck! I need the help of Kevin to get me out, much to everyone's amusement!

Getting stuck not withstanding, we all enjoyed ourselves, getting back on board in time for dinner.

Wednesday

We have a late breakfast today before setting the sails and making our way back past Clacton and Frinton, towards Brightlingsea. Frinton prides itself on its peaceful and genteel atmosphere, with no buses in the town centre and a Fish and Chip shop and pub only recently allowed. None of this is visible from the sea, however, only large grassy areas and its tower block of flats.

I lay on the deck in the sunshine watching the shore, I think to myself that we seem to be going backwards. This is a theory which is born out when Kevin puts the engine on so that we can reach our destination before running out of tide!

We eventually arrive around 1520. Near our resting-place is Cindery Island, which is covered at high tide. It is actually two islands, split across the middle. From its look, one could easily be persuaded that it was made from cinders! Local legend has it that a man who used to have to row across the river from the town split the island in two so that he could take a short cut. Probable nonsense, but a nice story nonetheless.

There is another story, this with more truth, that an eccentric American millionaire kept his ocean going private yacht, *Valfreya,* in the creek for twenty years in Victorian times. The yacht had steam up ready for instant sailing, day and night, winter and summer, but in all that time never left the harbour. Were the cinders from the boiler thrown onto Cindery Island?

The boys take the group ashore to play beach cricket while I remain on board to prepare dinner. They all return tired and happy for dinner and bed.

Thursday

Morning dawns with the weather 'grotty', to use the technical term. We have breakfast at 0800. although no one seems keen to get up! Eventually the group is coaxed into oilskin jackets to board the boats for a trip to Brightlingsea, shopping and playing in the park. (It's a hard life for some).

I remain on board and take the rare chance for a "Birdbath" before preparing lunch.

Everyone is back on board at 1315 and they quickly set about demolishing the waiting sandwiches. Once these have gone we have a competition to see if anyone can match Kevin's speed at eating a portion of Swiss roll. It's "On your marks, set, GO," but despite some valiant efforts no one can come close to Kev who downs his in one bite!

After lunch we motor to another beach. Although the wind has dropped, there is enough breeze for us to be surrounded by a number of small boats which mill around us like goldfish round bread, barely missing each other in their seeming excitement.

We make our way to the mouth of the Colne before dropping anchor once more and despatching everyone, except for me, of course, to the beach in the boats. They returned at 1730. When the wind started to pick up, we raised anchor and made our way back into the lee of Mersea Island for shelter.

After dinner the children are supposed to pack

their bags ready for tomorrow's departure. Some, keen to see home or just more organised than others, have already done this, however. We are all in bed for 2200 although it proves to be a noisy night.

Friday

Breakfast at 0800 today and then final packing. Sweeping up is done and then all the boxes are turned upside down to make sure that no socks have been left behind this week!

We up anchor at 0930 and make our way to West Mersea, the small town at the other end of the island, where we anchor once more for the last minute writing up of logs and handing out certificates. *Thalatta* will be based here for the weekend as a feature of the Mersea Regatta.

This week the going home is slightly different, as we have to wait for a fishing boat to arrive to take the kids ashore to be picked up by their parents. This done we are all ashore and have said our goodbyes by midday.

While waiting for Peter to come I look out across the water towards Tollesbury, where I can just make out the white shapes of the flats overlooking the Marina. This is, of course, a different view from that which I am accustomed from the other end of the Island. A year later there is to be fun and games had with fellow bargemen there.

It was a hot summer's evening and we were anchored in the Pyefleet not very far from where the *Edme* also lay. We spotted a twenty foot motor boat coming out from the St. Osyth direction carrying about half a dozen people. Before long it became apparent that Roger knew those on board, as he hailed them to come alongside.

I was talking on the telephone so did not take too much notice of what was going on until I saw Roger organising the children on the Hatch and I realised that they were armed with super soakers and water balloons. Clearly they were up to something!

The motor boat's bow nudged gently against our hull and the people on board prepared to be helped on deck. Instead of a warm welcome, however, they heard Roger cry,

"OK kids, let 'em have it."

With this a deluge of water balloons greeted our would be visitors who after token resistance retreated with some haste, to the more welcoming haven of the *Edme* where they promptly disappeared below.

Roger, knowing his friends well, was not fooled into believing that an easy victory had been secured, and busied the children with re-loading super soakers and water balloons in preparation for likely reprisals.

Sure enough, within a very few minutes the crew of the *Edme* returned in the boat, this time also armed with more super soakers and water balloons. Once they reached us they were soon up on our deck and letting fly with everything they had. Water bombs criss-crossed the deck and torrents of water sliced the air as kids of all ages joined a battle royal for nominal control of the barge. On our side one little boy seemed at a loss, with no weapon to use, so I called out,

"Hey, Kev, can you give Freddy a bucket?"

This Kevin duly did, filling it from our pump. The now delighted Freddy proceeded to join the battle. His efforts, however, temporarily rendered the combatants incapable with laughter as in his enthusiasm the bucket slipped out of his hands, and he threw this at the enemy rather than the water!

I watched for twenty minutes or so, whilst still

trying to talk on the phone, until either the ammunition supplies or the combatants were eventually exhausted and the *Edme* crew retreated to their own barge. Naturally our crew claimed this as a great victory and chided the opposition for running away. Some were keen to launch a counter attack. Sadly safety considerations meant that we could not take the children across for an assault of our own so we had to be content with the knowledge that both sides had had a thoroughly good time.

John Kemp   Co-founder E.C.S.T

Chapter Fifteen

The Cinque Ports and more from the past

Waldringfield School arrives on board in the late afternoon. We cast off as quickly as we can but given the late tide we can only motor as far as Osea Island where we anchor for our first night.

Today is just settling in and our highlight is the excitement generated, at least among the crew, when Roger catches THREE sea bass!

Tuesday

Breakfast at 0800 and then everyone joins in to raise the anchor. It is another beautiful day and we set the sails for the trip to Brightlingsea, just a few miles away. We are again the envy of all the "Yachties" who pass us and we parade our way up the river in our full glory!

Tired of showing off we anchor off Brightlingsea for the night. After dinner Roger takes me ashore in one of the boats to Mersea Stone. We meet friends Gwen and Rob in what must, to the casual observer, look like some clandestine meeting on the beach in the half-light. Do we exchange international secrets? arrange to collect illegal immigrants? Far better! We exchange last night's catch of Sea Bass for a bottle of wine!

Wednesday

Up for breakfast at 0800 on another lovely day. (Getting boring isn't it?)

After eating, everyone goes off to Brightlingsea to play, shop or explore. When they return one of the children asks about a sign she has seen referring to Brightlingsea being one of the "Cinque Ports" and Roger explains a little of their history:

"It is now generally believed that the Portsmen

138

first came together informally, during the 11th Century, to regulate the important herring-fair held each year at Great Yarmouth. This was not just a common economic interest but also a strategic one, as the Ports were on a coast constantly open to attack and controlled the important sea routes across the English Channel.

The earliest known charter granting rights in common to the Cinque Ports dates from 1260. It was probably Edward the Confessor (1042-1066) who first set about replacing the Saxon mercenary fleet with one drawn from the five ports, with the help of nearby coastal towns and villages. In return for the granting of privileges, Edward was able to muster a fleet to maintain the important transportation links to Normandy and to protect his kingdom from attack. By the reign of Henry II (1154-1189), the towns were already known collectively as the *"Cinque Ports"*.

At first, charters giving privileges were granted to the Ports individually, since they retained their right to act independently, in matters not of mutual concern, and separate charters were generally considered to be more effective. However, by the middle of the 12th Century, the Court of Shepway had been established with jurisdiction over all of the Ports. Over the next 100 years or so, rights first granted, separately, to the individual members of the Confederation became consolidated in joint charters.

Some of the most significant of these rights were the right to levy local taxes, to hold their own courts and to punish offenders. There was also the privilege of den and strand, that is, the right to dry and mend their nets and to organise a large and lucrative Herring Fair each year, in order to sell their catch, at the mouth of the River Yare in Norfolk;

The name Cinque Ports comes from the Norman French for five and originally comprised the five ports of Hastings, Romney, Hythe, Dover and Sandwich. Under the system called 'ship service', the Ports were required to supply 57 ships, each with a crew of 21 men and a boy, for 15 days every year. These ships were not just for fighting but also to transport the King and his troops or courtiers to anywhere in Europe.

'Ship service' was an onerous duty and the five original head ports enlisted the help of neighbouring towns and villages, which were known as members or limbs, to help them fulfil their quotas of ships and crew. Some of the limbs were merely small villages and hamlets and these non-corporate members negotiated directly, with their head port, to provide ships and men, in return for the right to share in the privileges granted to the head port. Other limbs were more substantial communities and were granted their own charters by the Crown, thus becoming corporate members. At one time, there were 23 limbs covering an extensive area from Seaford, in the west, to Brightlingsea on the Essex coast"

With that explanation we all pause for a rest!

After lunch we set sail for Bradwell where we settle so that everyone can once more go ashore. This time to play on the beach. After dinner Kev decides to up anchor and move us the short distance to a better location. Once settled again, the children do some crabbing before lights out.

Thursday

We make a late start, as we have not far to go. Breakfast is at 0900 and then it's up anchor and we make our way under full sail to Maldon.

For the walkers on the sea wall as we pass my

home village of Tollesbury, we must be a magnificent sight, red sails fully set and black wooden hull gleaming in the bright sunshine; a sight only bettered by being on board looking back at them, for we at least are cool out on the water. Those on land have recently experienced some of the hottest temperatures on record. 100°F last weekend! We tie up at Maldon about 1730 and after we have dinner I slip off home for the night.

Friday

I am dutifully back on board by 0730, only to find that no one is yet up. I prepare breakfast for 0800 and this has the desired effect! After eating, it is a good clear up and clean all round ready for the parents to collect the group at 1130. Then it's off home and look forward to a "Murphy's" up the British Legion.

Monday

It is August Bank holiday and I arrive on board, with all the provisions at 0900. We have time to stow everything and enjoy a brew in the traditional "Calm before the Storm" before, an hour later, our crew for the week arrive from the Norwich School. This, believe it or not, is in Norwich, and features, if briefly, in the recorded history of our barge.

Joe Lucas, a Manningtree Sailorman and occasional drinking companion of Roger, recalled his time aboard the *Thalatta* in a documentary film of 1973. And thus his experiences are handed down to us.

As a young man in 1943, Joe joined the barge at Lowestoft and made his first trip on board from here down to London to pick up a cargo of 700 Cwt of maize, which was carried up to Norwich. Neither the time of year nor the time taken is recorded, though we do know from later records that each trip would have taken a day or more depending on tide and weather.

Joe also recalls that he made a number of trips with cow cake to Mistley, a common trip for barges at the time.

In the 1930s and beyond, Brooks of Mistley provided much trade for the barge fleet, bringing in the raw materials to the quay for their famous "Cow Cubes".

Once this animal feed was mixed and ready it was tried out on the trial herd of cattle kept at the nearby "Trinity Farm". If each batch was satisfactory it would be sold to farms throughout East Anglia, being reputed to improve the health and yield of the cattle.

Pictures of Mistley Quay taken at the time show half a dozen or more barges at a time waiting to be unloaded, often either by hand or by simple rope and tackle.

In his narrative, Joe Lucas relates how it was common to take wheat up to Green's Mill at Brantham, a trip requiring the barge Skipper to negotiate passage under the humped back bridge at Catawade. There was so little clearance that barges would anchor up on the ebbing tide with their nose as far under the bridge as possible. As soon as the incoming tide lifted the barge clear of the bottom, passage would be made under the bridge with about three inches clearance (according to Joe). Once through to the other side there would now be sufficient water for the Skipper to make the rest of the journey at his leisure.

Film taken for the documentary shows how faithfully *Thalatta* has retained her appearance from her days in trade, though her paintwork may be a little cleaner and brighter today and she had her wheel house removed a few years ago now.

We set out at 1100 and make our way out to Osea Island where we anchor in time for the school children to enjoy the packed lunch which they had brought. One of the Mums has sent chocolate brownies and flapjacks. Very nice indeed. We all sit on deck and enjoy our feast. We spend the day lazing around and enjoying the sunshine.

After dinner it is the usual first night hammock demonstration followed by lights out at 2140.

Tuesday

The last Tuesday of the season. It is flat calm when, after breakfast we up anchor and make our way to Brightlingsea. As there is no breeze today we have to use the engine all the way, of course.

After lunch Kevin goes ashore to Brightlingsea whilst the children are taken to the opposite side of the river, to Mersea Island. Roger is bait digging. I remain on board and make cheesecake for this evening. After dinner the children spend the evening crabbing before log keeping and lights out at 2200.

Wednesday

A good day today. We have everyone polishing brass in the morning. There is a surprising amount of brass on the barge trimming on the ship's wheel, the compass and skylights-so there is a lot to be done. It is, however, well worth the effort when the sun gleams off the polished metal, contrasting with the blue of the hatch cover or the wood of the wheel!

There is enough breeze today to allow us to do plenty of sailing, much to everyone's enjoyment. It would be a good idea perhaps for me to describe how we 'set sail'.

Roger organises our crew ready to set the sails. First will be the fors'l. The children are lined up along the deck while the halliard for raising the sail is sorted out. Everyone grabs hold and Roger calls out,

"Are you ready?"

"Yes, Roger," comes the inevitable reply.

"Right then. Two, six, heave. Two, six, heave"

As the halliard is heaved the sail gradually rises up from its resting-place by the anchor winch until it is fully deployed, running from the bow to the mainmast and permanently attached to the fore horse by its traveller.

Now it is time to raise the mains'l. The wooden sheet block, which holds the sheets, (that is the ropes that pull out the sail), is slowly drawn from its place at the base of the main mast, back to the main horse where it is attached by the iron ring known as the traveller.

"Right. Everyone to the stern, behind the horse," Roger orders.

Once our sailors are in place they take a firm grip of the sheet paid out from the block.

"OK as before. Two, six, heave. Two, six, heave."

While the crew heave, Roger uses the winch by the mast to slowly release the brails, that is the ropes looped round the sail to gather it together when not in use. The top three of these brails are known as peaks, but now we are getting too technical!

Once the mains'l has been fully extended the sheet is secured on the block with the customary figure eight, before being coiled clockwise on the deck by the horse.

Today we are also raising the jib, so it is all hands amidships, and repeat the procedure as before until the jib rises to its place above the fors'l. Since the jib has been deployed, Kevin gets some of the youngsters to help him raise the mizzen sail which will balance the extra canvas of the jib. We are now ready for, and enjoy, some fine sailing!

144

For some however, despite the excellent sailing, the highlight of the day is watching a seal swimming round our stern. After lunch, taken on deck, of course, the children go off to do some swimming before returning for a demonstration of knots.

After dinner it is an ideal crabbing evening, although just how many were caught I cannot tell. Not that it really mattered to anyone very much as everybody had such a good time. Not sure what the crabs thought about it but I think most of them got a free meal!

Thursday

Another nice day, we have breakfast early at 0800 before the children go to Brightlingsea for the last time this season. It is now starting to feel very "end of term" for us but we cannot let the youngsters feel this, as it is possibly the high spot of their school year!

After lunch we up anchor and make our way to Osea where we settle for the night.

Friday

We make our way back to Maldon where, after mooring, we say good bye to our charges before tidying up and going ashore. Reading through the "Crews logbook" for the week we see that, although it may have been a quiet week for us, the kids had thoroughly enjoyed themselves as usual. We see written,

"A fun, action packed day."

"We went crabbing and starboard team won 26-21. It was a great day!"

"We left after a great week on the *Thalatta*."

Comments such as these make all the hard work well worth while.

This is "end of term" for me. Peter has now returned to work and fortunately is fit enough for us to go on our holiday to my favourite spot, Fuschl, just outside Salzburg, in Austria. (*Peter's note: Such is Rita's ingenuity and dedication to the cause of water fighting she even manages to engineer an ambush at our Hotelier's son's birthday party with water balloons and super soakers. The balcony of the Hotel Stefanihof makes a dangerous nest for a Rita with water bombs! You can guess which one of us had eventually to be sacrificially half drowned, much to the enjoyment of the young partygoers!*)

I have found it a long hard summer trying to balance my job on the barge with looking after my husband. The time away has caused frictions from time to time, and two weeks together does much to smooth things over.

Epilogue

After Holidays

So we are back at Wolverstone Marina for the last 'day sails' of the year. The routine is the same as at the beginning of the season with me collecting the food from Tollesbury and bringing it on board.

I have various helpers during another enjoyable week. Robin, a friend from the village comes on board and Kevin is brave enough to allow him a long turn at the wheel. Robin resembles a dog with two tails for weeks afterwards!

The week passes quickly and enjoyably, although we are perhaps a little sad when the Friday evening brings an end to our active season.

Although the sailing season ends with the last of the day sails it does not by any means bring an end to the work. Everything, which we did at the start of the season now, has to be done in reverse!

The first task, of course, is to get the old girl back to Maldon (*Thalatta,* that is). Once safely "at home" we can begin the work of cleaning and stowing all our gear. Sails have to be taken down and safely stowed below, the mast is lowered and everything made secure. Roger and I work on board for another fortnight, though Kevin is busy on board at various times throughout the winter.

Spring again

After what as always seems an endless winter we all start back once more at the beginning of February, keen and eager for the new season.

There is much work to be done again before we can sail this year, as our electrics need more attention. Consequently from time to time we are trying to work by the glimmer of the 12-Volt lighting while switches and wiring are replaced.

I am now in possession of a new gas powered fridge for the Galley, though not as yet a freezer. Still, never mind. (If the weather for the first trip is anything to go by a freezer could be the last of our needs, but that is another story).

As part of our preparation we spend some time in dry dock having work done to those bits not normally accessible and the boys do much filling, painting and drilling. I make much tea and develop into a reasonable ship's painter.

Once we have finished in dry dock we spend a short time at Maylandsea, where we have a new pin fitted to the rudder. We also have one of the leeboards repaired.

So all is eventually (nearly) ready. At the beginning of April I spend a couple of hours going round Tesco's once more and husband Peter helps me load the provisions on board on the Saturday morning, ready for the first trip which will start our adventures anew for this year.

(Peter's note: I have only seen the barge once before, this season, and that was when she was in dry dock. When we load the provisions on board, on a dull cool morning, Thalatta is in total contrast to the apparent jumble of assorted odds and ends which greeted me on that occasion.

To load, I have to transfer a score or more of plastic carrier bags from the boot of our car on the quayside, up the gangplank of the barge next to ours, across the deck and then hand them over to Rita on Thalatta's deck. This all accomplished, Rita goes down below and I have to kneel on the deck and pass the bags down the forward hatch to Rita's upstretched hands below. The whole exercise is probably equivalent to about an hour in the gym!

Transfer complete I go below and try to avoid standing on the newly painted ceiling as we put the stores away. The whole barge is now painted, scrubbed and polished (except for the brass!) clean and shiny. She looks like a beautiful lady about to go out on the town.

Whilst the appearance of everything may have changed since the last time I was on board, the atmosphere has not, and we are warmly greeted by Kevin when he comes back. I am graciously allowed to make coffee. I am however initially bamboozled by the kettle, which now seems to work by being plugged into the electric!

Coffee and loading complete we make our way home. Two days later, Rita and the boys are off on the first cruise of the year. The weather is cold and squally but they do see a flamingo off Fingringhoe! (I have to be content with seeing my first swallows of the summer).

The Most Important Part Of The Barge

Appendix One
Definitions

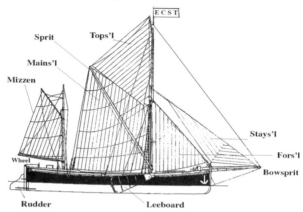

The following are non-technical definitions of some words and expressions used around barges which may not be familiar to fellow "landlubbers".

Bob   *Flag flown from the top of the main mast bearing the colours and or name of the owner.*

Boomie   *Ketch rigged barge. i.e. with a boom rather than the now more common sprit.*

Brails   *Ropes used to secure the sails when they are furled.*

Ceiling   *The caulked floor of the hold.*

Cleat   *Two pronged device around which a rope can be secured.*

Coiled Springs   *The Crew when they are prepared to leap into action at a moment's notice, despite giving the appearance of being asleep or close to it!*

Dressing the Sails   *Simply painting them with the preservative, which gives them their traditional red colour. Once made from a variety of unsavoury ingredients, this is now bought as a proprietry product "off the shelf".*

Gybe   *The bringing of the sails from one side of the barge* *to the other as the heading is altered to bring the wind from one quarter to another. Swinging the sails across the deck. Dangerous to the unwary. On Thalatta such a manoeuvre is usually preceded by a call of "Leo" as warning. There are also red lines painted denoting the danger areas fore and aft.*

Halliard   *Rope used to pull up the sails, e.g. Jib or Fors'l*

Heads   *Toilets, see text for origin.*

Horse   *The wooden (on some barges, iron) beam across the barge fore and aft, fore sails and main sails being attached by a large metal ring. Also makes a good seat! (under 'Gybe')*

Keelson   *Wooden or (in Thalatta) steel beam running from bow to stern forming the internal backbone of the barge.*

Mulie   *Barge with sprit for the mainsail and boom for the mizzen.*

Sheet   *Rope used for pulling out the sails. On the mains'l this is attached to the sheet block, which in turn can be hooked to the traveller.*

Sprit   *attached to the main mast, rising at an angle and supporting the main sail. Hence spritsail rigged.*

Sprittie   *spritsail rigged barge.*

Stackie   *Barge loaded with a "stack" of hay or straw protruding above deck. Sometimes built a little broader in the beam to facilitate this.*

Traveller   *Ring, running across the horse carrying the sheet block.*

Transom   *Square cut end of the barge, In construction this holds the sides of the barge together. Customarily these have brightly decorative paintwork except when the barge is in mourning.*

Vang   *(pronounced wang). Wire rigged from the end of the sprit to the deck. Used to keep the sprit under control.*

151

Appendix Two
Friends of 'Thalatta'

The East Coast Sail Trust is a registered charity (no.263100) and as such has to comply with strict conditions as laid down by the Charity Commission. *'Thalatta'* celebrated her 90th year in 1996 and has an exemplary safety record built up by the late John Kemp and Jane Benham M.B.E., who were amongst the originators of the Trust. This Trust is currently run by a body of four appointed trustees. These trustees are supported by an appeal committee of two, a booking secretary and a crew of three responsible for the safe operation of the barge.

All staff, whether working in a voluntary or paid capacity, are committed to maintaining the high reputation of the Trust to the benefit of young people from all sectors of the Community.

How you can Help:

'Thalatta' needs constant maintenance and attention to keep her in a seaworthy and safe condition, and the East Coast Sail Trust needs assistance, both financial and practical. By becoming a 'Friend' you will be helping to support the upkeep of the barge. Also you will receive regular newsletters updating you with the Trust's and barge's activities.

As a 'Friend' you will receive priority invitations to visit the barge when she is open at Maldon, Woodbridge, St Katherine's Dock (London), and other various locations around the East Coast. You will also receive prior notice for the opportunity to sail on the barge. Day sails are arranged at various times during the season (April to September), and there are also occasional weekend sailing opportunities to and from London.

As well as your financial assistance, the Trust is always keen to hear from Friends who have skills which could be of use to the maintenance of the barge and Trust. This could include a practical skill such as shipwrighting; or a willingness to help staff the barge when she is open to the public.

Being a charity, the East Coast Sail Trust is able to receive regular donations by means of covenants/gift aids which have the benefit of providing the trust with a refund of income tax at standard rate, at no additional cost to you. As a covenantor you will receive tax relief at your highest marginal rate.

Appendix Three
Surviving Barges

The Barge Trust list the following as being 'Active' as of 2003

ADIEU
Builder: F.W. Horlock at Mistley 1929
79 reg tons. Private yacht berthed at St. Katherine's Dock.

ALICE
Builder: Cook's of Wivenhoe 1954 as a lighter. Rebuilt as a sailing barge by Owen Emerson in 1994. She is now based in London and owned and operated by Looking Glass Charters at Butlers Wharf.

ARDWINA
Builder: Orvis and Fuller at Ipswich 1909. 66 reg tons. Owned by Ardwina Limited she is based at St. Katherine's Dock and used for promotional work.

BERIC
Sold to Newcastle a few years ago to become a pub. In August 2003 she was sold to a new Maldon based owner. Now she is refitting at Fullbridge.

BETULA
Built in Holland in 1924 of steel she was bought by Eddie Smith in 1996 and rebuilt as a Thames sailing barge with gear from the Vicunia, Anglia, Sara and Venture. She is a private yacht and operates from Pin Mill in Suffolk.

CABBY
Built at Rochester in 1928 by the London and Rochester Trading Company this 76 ton barge was the last wooden barge built and remained in the ownership of her builders as they became Crescent Shipping, and later part of the Hays Group, until sold to new owners in Maldon in 2002. She remains engaged in promotional charter work.

CENTAUR
Built in 1895, the work of J & H Cann, generally regarded by many bargemen as the finest barge builders of all. She traded under sail alone until the late 1950's when she became a timber lighter at Heybridge. Rerigged for charter work in 1966 she was bought by the TBSC in 1974.

153

CYGNET

A half size barge she was built in 1881 by Curel for use trading to small farm creeks. Although half the length of a full size barge she registers only 16 tons which is roughly a quarter of the capacity of a fullsize barge. Owned by Mica Brown she is sailed single handed by skipper Des Kalizewski.

EDME

Built in 1898 she is another example of the work of J & H Cann. She ended her trading career as a lighter and was restored at Maldon before she was purchased and rigged out by the Harman consortium in 1992. Based at her skipper Andy Harman's St. Osyth yard she is now used for charter work and carried a cargo in 2002.

ETHEL ADA

Built at Paglesham by Shuttleworth in 1903 this little barge was rebuilt by the late Joe Dunnet in the 1980's at Pin Mill. Now privately owned and underway again after several years laid up.

GLADYS

Another product of Cann's yard at Harwich in 1901. Owned at Ipswich by Cranfields she was a trading motor barge until 1974 when she was re-rigged and is recognised by the Sunblest Bread symbol in her topsail. Used for company promotional events out of St. Katherine's Dock.

GRETA

A 46 reg ton barge built at Brightlingsea in 1892 and now based at Faversham in Kent. Owner Steve Norris charters the barge especially in the Kent area.

HENRY

Based at Faversham she is near the end of a lengthy restoration and has been underway this year and will hopefully be regularly active now.

HYDROGEN

Built at Rochester in 1906 this big 98 reg ton coaster is now operated by Topsail Charters Limited of Maldon where she is based and carries large charter parties on day trips as well as operating in London and other parts of the east coast.

KITTY

Another Cann barge built like Centaur in 1895 at Harwich she is 65 reg tons. Built for the famous Horlock family of Mistley she featured their distinctive sheer line. Rerigged at Maldon in 1964 she operated for many years under the command and ownership of John Fairbrother sailing without an engine. Sold to the south coast she became a floating restaurant before current use as a charter barge based in the Solent area.

LADY DAPHNE

Built in 1923 at Rochester this big 85 reg ton coaster was rerigged for Taylor Woodrow as a centre piece for their St. Katherine's Dock development from where she now works as a charter barge owned by Elisabeth and Michael Mainelli.

LADY JEAN

A sister ship of Lady Daphne built by Shorts at Rochester from the same plans, she was once renamed Sir Alan Herbert and owned by the East Coast Sail Trust. Now owned by Iden and Sheena Wickings and used as a private yacht she annually voyages to France from her Maldon base.

MARJORIE

Built in Ipswich in 1902 by Orvis this 56 reg ton coaster was a fully rigged sailing barge in trade until 1961, when she became a charter barge at Maldon where she was based for many years, also being used as a private yacht. In the 1970s she was purchased by Albert Groom and is now owned by barrister Simon Devonshire and restored by Robert Deards who is her skipper. Based in Robert's yard at Hoo or St. Katherine's Dock.

MAY

A 57 reg ton product of Cann's yard at Harwich in 1891 she was owned by Cranfields of Ipswich until 1964 when she was bought by Tate and Lyle's subsidiary Silvertown Services. She once went to Canada for the Olympics (by ship not under sail!) and these days operates as a charter barge.

MIROSA

Built by Howard of Maldon in1892 this 49 reg ton barge was a stackie that carried straw to London from Essex farms. Another barge to survive because she was a timber lighter at Heybridge Basin, she was rerigged in 1967 and since 1977 has been owned by Peter Dodds and based in his yard at Faversham. Sailed without an engine she is used as a charter barge and as a private yacht.

MONTREAL

Built Sittingbourne, 1902 as swim head lighter, bought by Owen Emerson 1970 and rigged. Sold to Iden Wickings as a yacht, bought by Vadim Jean, 1996 and berthed at St. Mary's Church Mooring, Battersea. Underway in 2002 and now lying at Hoo.

NELLIE

Only 43 reg tons, this river barge was built in 1901 at Faversham and is now rigged as a stumpy with no topmast. After years as a houseboat she was restored in 1985 at Maldon where she is still based and is a floating home to owner Diane Montgomery.

PHOENICIAN

Built at Sittingbourne in 1922 this 81 reg ton coaster was built for Captain Alf Horlock who raced her successfully in the 1920s/30s. Rerigged from a motor barge in 1973 by Albert Groom she is now owned by Grant Littler.

PUDGE

A sister ship of Cabby completed 6 years earlier in 1922 this 67 reg ton barge was traded by her builders the London and Rochester Trading Company until 1968 when sold to the Thames Barge Sailing Club and rigged again. She has been sailed as a charter barge to raise funds for barge restoration since 1982, based at Maldon. Extensive restoration work started in 1997 and continues.

REMINDER

Built by Horlocks at Mistley of steel in 1929 she was a fast racing barge and traded as a motor barge until 1974 when Roger Beckett restored her to sail, since when she has chartered out of Maldon where she is today operated by Topsail Charters.

REPERTOR

Another steel barge built at Mistley by Horlocks in 1924 of 69 reg tons, she was restored to sail in 1977. She is now owned by Gordon Pollock of Faversham and operates as a charter barge, like her younger sister Reminder.

THALATTA

A big coaster she is of 76 reg tons. She is owned by the East Coast Sail Trust a registered charity founded by John Kemp in 1971. Always Maldon based she takes school children sailing as a sail training ship.

THISTLE

Built of steel in Scotland in 1895 she was restored to sail in 1988 and is now based at Maldon and owned by Topsail Charters Limited. Luxuriously converted for charter work, complete with a cockpit in the main hold, she is licensed to carry 50 passengers.

VICTOR

Built at Ipswich in 1895. Ended her trading days as a motor barge and rerigged by Owen Emerson in 1974, she became a charter barge and was sold to Nick Briggs in 1995. Now based on the Solent or at Butler's Wharf in London. She is licensed to carry 40 passengers.

WYVENHOE

Built of steel in 1898. Rerigged by Richard Walsh in 1984 and sold to her present owners 11 years ago, since when she has been based in St. Katherine's Dock. She is used for static and sailing charters.

XYLONITE

Built of steel as BX by Horlocks at Mistley in 1926. Rigged out for charter holidays in the 1970's she later lay alongside the Prospect of Whitby pub at Wapping until 1985, when the Cirdan Sailing Trust acquired her as a youth training ship. She has been based at Maldon for the past 18 years. Skippered by trust member Richard Titchener, she has established herself as a very fast racing barge.